TALK, DON'T YELL

Nine Proven Tools for Mindful Parenting,
Gentle Discipline, and Raising Emotionally
Secure, Respectful Kids Without Yelling

ELLIS CARTER

TABLE OF CONTENTS

INTRODUCTION

Everyone yells sometimes.

Yes, even that Instagram mom with the beautifully organized home and children who appear to communicate only in inside voices and grateful affirmations. Yes, even your friend who's studying to be a child psychologist. Yes, even me—the person writing a book called *Talk, Don't Yell.*

I want to acknowledge something right off the bat—the fact that you've picked up this book means you care deeply about how you show up for your kids. The parent who doesn't care doesn't feel guilty. The parent who doesn't care doesn't stay awake replaying that moment when their voice escalated and their child's eyes widened. The parent who doesn't care doesn't seek out better ways.

You care. So much that it hurts.

Here's what I've learned from years of research and countless conversations with parents just like you: Yelling isn't a moral failing or a character flaw. It's a nervous system response to overwhelm. It's what happens when our prehistoric brain— designed to handle saber-toothed tigers and food scarcity— attempts to process 47 interruptions while making dinner, three separate homework crises, a work email that won't stop pinging, and a child who has chosen this exact moment to test whether no really means no for the 17th time today.

Your brain, in its infinite wisdom, reaches for the evolutionary shortcut: Make a loud noise. Assert dominance. Gain immediate compliance.

It works—sort of. For a minute. And then comes the aftermath: the guilt, the little face looking up at you, the internal promise that "tomorrow will be different," the creeping fear that maybe you're just not cut out for this most important job.

I call this the yell-regret cycle, and it's as common as sippy cups under the couch. This cycle isn't just emotionally exhausting— it's neurologically draining. Each loop reinforces neural pathways that make the next cycle more likely. It's not your fault. But it is something you can change.

The Science Behind Gentle Parenting

The approaches in this book aren't just feel-good philosophies. They're backed by decades of research into attachment, neurobiology, and child development. When we parent from a place of connection rather than control, we're not just being "nice"—we're literally shaping our children's brain architecture in ways that promote emotional regulation, resilience, and secure attachment.

Studies show that children raised with authoritative parenting—high warmth combined with clear limits— demonstrate better outcomes across nearly every measure of well-being: academic achievement, emotional regulation, peer relationships, and resistance to high-risk behaviors.

But here's the part most researchers don't talk about: implementing authoritative parenting is really freaking hard when you're operating on four hours of sleep and your toddler just colored on the wall with permanent marker. The gap between what we know we should do and what we actually do in stressful moments isn't about knowledge—it's about nervous system regulation.

Your Parenting Pressure Points

Before we dive into tools, let's take a moment to understand your unique parenting landscape. Every parent has specific triggers that make yelling more likely:

- **Sensory overwhelm triggers**: when noise, mess, or physical sensation becomes too much

- **Time pressure triggers**: when running late or managing tight schedules

- **Behavior button-pushers**: those specific behaviors that seem designed to make you lose it

- **Resource depletion triggers**: when you're hungry, exhausted, or emotionally drained

- **History echoes**: when your child's behavior activates your own childhood experiences

Take a moment to consider which of these resonates most strongly for you. Understanding your personal triggers isn't about making excuses—it's about gaining the self-awareness that makes change possible.

The Nine-Tool Roadmap

This book offers nine practical tools that work together as a system. You don't need to implement them all perfectly or at the same time. Think of them as instruments in an orchestra—each one contributes something unique, and together they create something beautiful.

Here's what we'll cover:

1. **The Reset Button**: managing your triggers before they manage you

2. **The Respect Loop**: how to model the behavior you want to see

3. **The Calm Script**: what to say instead of yelling

4. **The Boundary Builder**: how to say no with love (and mean it)

5. **The Conversation Catcher**: creating safe space for real talks

6. **The Emotional Coach**: teaching kids to handle big feelings

7. **The Routine Reset**: designing peaceful days that prevent chaos

8. **The Repair Ritual**: how to rebuild connection after a blow-up

9. **The Parent Recharge Plan**: how to stay regulated and show up with confidence

As we explore each tool, I promise to be practical, not preachy. I won't suggest elaborate techniques that require you to suddenly have more time, money, or patience than you currently possess. These tools are designed for real parents in real homes with real limitations.

The journey we're about to begin isn't about becoming perfect. It's about becoming present. It's about breaking the cycle of yelling that leaves everyone feeling awful and replacing it with something that works better for you and your kids.

You've already taken the first step by acknowledging that you want something different. That's the hardest part. From here, we move forward together, one tool at a time.

Tool 1:
The Reset Button—Managing Your Triggers Before They Manage You

I t's 5:47 p.m. You've been up since 5:30 a.m. Your brain feels like it's been wrapped in a scratchy wool blanket. You're making dinner while helping with homework, while answering work emails, while mentally cataloging the mountain of laundry that somehow reproduced itself overnight. Your 7-year-old has asked the same question 14 times. Your 4-year-old just spilled milk across the kitchen floor that you cleaned 20 minutes ago.

And then it happens.

Something in you snaps. Your voice rises to a volume that surprises even you. The kitchen falls silent. Your children's faces register shock, then hurt. Your heart sinks as familiar guilt floods your system. You've done it again.

Welcome to what I call the yell-regret cycle. If you've picked up this book, chances are you know this cycle intimately. You're not alone. In fact, you're in the majority—studies suggest that up to 90% of parents report yelling at their children regularly, and almost all feel terrible about it afterward[1].

Understanding the Yell-Regret Cycle

Let's break down what's happening in your brain during these moments. When you're triggered, your body's threat-detection system—the amygdala—activates what neuroscientists call the hypothalamic-pituitary-adrenal axis, or HPA axis. This triggers a cascade of stress hormones through your body, including cortisol and adrenaline. These chemicals prepare you for fight, flight, or freeze responses.

This biological reaction made perfect sense for our ancestors facing predators or tribal warfare. It makes much less sense when you're trying to get a kindergartner to put on their shoes before the school bus arrives. But your body doesn't know the difference between a tiger and a tantrum—it just knows threat.

As stress hormones flood your system, something remarkable happens to your brain architecture. Your prefrontal cortex—the rational, planning, executive function part of your brain—temporarily goes offline. Simultaneously, your limbic system—the emotional, reactive part—takes over. Scientists call this "amygdala hijacking," but parents might recognize it as that moment when you hear yourself yelling and think, *Who is this person?*

The worst part? After you yell, you experience a brief neurochemical "release" that feels oddly satisfying for about 2.7 seconds. This surge can mistakenly reinforce the yelling

---

[1] Wang & Kenny, 2013

behavior at a subconscious level, making it more likely you'll react the same way next time.

Then comes the aftermath. The cognitive part of your brain comes back online and surveys the damage. You see your child's hurt expression. You feel the tension in the room. The shame and guilt flood in, along with promises to yourself that next time will be different. But when the next trigger inevitably comes, the cycle often repeats.

This cycle is remarkably resistant to willpower alone. You can't simply decide not to yell and expect that decision to hold up under extreme stress. What you can do is learn to interrupt the cycle much earlier, before your brain chemistry takes the wheel.

The reset button is your first and most fundamental tool because it addresses the root cause of yelling: your own nervous system activation. When you can regulate yourself, everything else becomes possible.

Trigger Mapping: Know Your Personal Activation Points

Not all parents yell in the same situations. Your trigger points are as unique as your fingerprint, shaped by your temperament, childhood experiences, values, and current life circumstances.

Let's identify your personal trigger map. Physical triggers often form the foundation. These include sensory overwhelm—the cumulative effect of noise, mess, and physical discomfort that can push even the most patient parent to the edge. Sleep deprivation is another major physical trigger; research shows that just one night of poor sleep can reduce emotional regulation capacity by up to 30%[2]. Other physical triggers include hunger (giving rise to the term "hangry parenting"), physical pain, and hormonal fluctuations that can intensify emotional responses.

Time-based triggers create pressure cooker situations where yelling becomes more likely. The morning rush, when everyone needs to be fed, dressed, and out the door by a specific time, ranks high on most parents' trigger lists. Bedtime battles are another common flashpoint, as everyone's resources are depleted at day's end. Transitions between activities, especially for children who struggle with change, can become trigger minefields. Deadlines and time pressure of any kind compress your tolerance for frustration. And perhaps most significantly, end-of-day fatigue—that period from 5 to 8 p.m., which many parents call "the witching hours," creates the perfect storm of depleted resources and high demands.

Behavioral triggers are specific actions from your children that seem scientifically designed to make you lose your cool. Whining ranks near the top for most parents; studies show that the particular pitch of a child's whine activates stress responses in the parental brain[3]. Not listening or requiring multiple repetitions taps into feelings of invisibility or disrespect. Sibling fighting forces you into the exhausting role of referee. Defiance and backtalk can feel like a direct challenge to your authority. And dangerous behavior triggers primal protective instincts that can erupt as yelling.

Emotional triggers cut closest to our core. Feeling disrespected activates shame responses that can be particularly difficult to

---

[2] Tomaso et al., 2020
[3] Li et al., 2018

regulate. Feeling incompetent as a parent triggers deep insecurities about our worthiness. Feeling trapped—a common experience in the relentless demands of parenting—can trigger panic responses. Feeling manipulated by a child's behavior provokes defensive reactions. And perhaps most powerfully, being reminded of your own childhood—particularly if you experienced harsh parenting yourself—can trigger reflexive responses before you're even conscious of the connection.

Take some time to reflect on which triggers affect you most strongly. When you know what pushes you toward the edge, you can prepare specific strategies for those moments.

Understanding your triggers isn't about making excuses—it's about gaining the self-awareness that makes change possible. By mapping your triggers, you're developing the recognition skills that precede any meaningful change.

Rapid Calm Techniques: Your Emergency Reset Kit

Now for the practical part: What do you do when you feel yourself heating up? Here's your emergency reset kit—techniques specifically designed to work within seconds to minutes, even in the chaos of active parenting.

The 4-6-8 Breath Reset (30 seconds)

This isn't just any breathing technique. The specific pattern of inhaling for 4 counts, holding for 6 counts, and exhaling for 8 counts activates your parasympathetic nervous system, essentially hitting the "calm" button on your body's stress response. The lengthened exhale is particularly effective at reducing heart rate and blood pressure quickly.

When you're triggered, your breathing naturally becomes shallow and rapid, further signaling danger to your nervous system. By deliberately extending your exhale to be longer than your inhale, you send a powerful message to your brain: "I am safe. There is no emergency here."

Practice this pattern during calm moments so it becomes automatic during stress. Even one round of 4-6-8 breathing can measurably reduce stress hormones in your bloodstream. Three rounds can completely shift your physiological state.

Sarah, a mother of three, describes her experience: "The breathing feels almost magical sometimes. I'll be about to completely lose it with my kids, and I'll force myself to do the 4-6-8 pattern. By the third breath, my shoulders have dropped from around my ears, and I can think again. My kids have actually started to recognize when I'm doing it and will sometimes remind me, 'Mom, do your special breathing!'"

The Physical Pattern Interrupt (15 seconds)

Your body and brain operate in constant feedback loops. Your emotional state affects your physical posture, but the reverse is also true—your physical posture affects your emotional state. This technique leverages that bidirectional relationship to create rapid change.

When triggered, your body assumes a threat posture: shoulders raised, jaw clenched, breath held, weight shifted forward. By deliberately changing this posture, you can send a powerful "safety" signal to your nervous system.

The sequence is simple: Press your feet firmly into the floor to ground yourself. Roll your shoulders back and down to release the protective hunching. Straighten your posture to counteract the collapse of stress. Place one hand on your heart in a self-soothing gesture that activates oxytocin release. Then, take one deliberate breath to reset your respiratory pattern.

This sequence short-circuits the physical posture of stress and sends a powerful signal to your brain that you're safe. It works because your brain constantly monitors your body position for clues about your emotional state—changing your posture can literally change your mind.

Michael, father of twins, shares: "I used to clench my fists when I got angry, which just made me feel more aggressive. Now, I deliberately open my hands and place one on my heart when I feel myself getting triggered. Something about that open-hand posture helps me feel more open to my kids rather than closed off and defensive."

The Name-It-To-Tame-It Technique (10 seconds)

This remarkably simple technique comes from Dr. Dan Siegel's research on interpersonal neurobiology. The act of labeling an emotion activates your prefrontal cortex, helping it stay online rather than letting your limbic system take complete control[4].

When you feel yourself escalating, mentally or quietly label what you're feeling: "This is frustration." Notice where you feel it in your body: "Tight chest, clenched jaw." Acknowledge the trigger: "I'm triggered by the repeated interruptions."

Neuroscience research shows that simply naming emotions reduces their intensity by up to 50%[5]. The labeling process creates what scientists call "psychological distance," enough

[4] Siegel, 2021
[5] Levy-Gigi & Shamay-Tsoory, 2022

space between you and the emotion to prevent complete identification with it. You shift from "I am angry" to "I am experiencing anger," a subtle but powerful distinction.

Elena, mother of a strong-willed preschooler, explains: "Naming my emotions helps me remember that feelings are temporary visitors, not my whole identity. When I think *I'm enraged*, I feel out of control. When I think *I'm experiencing frustration right now*, I somehow feel more capable of managing it."

The 5-4-3-2-1 Grounding Exercise (60 seconds)

When you're really spinning out, this sensory technique pulls you back to the present by engaging all five senses. The process is straightforward: Notice 5 things you can see around you, paying attention to details and colors. Acknowledge 4 things you can physically touch, feeling the textures and temperatures. Listen for 3 distinct sounds in your environment, from obvious to subtle. Identify 2 things you can smell or like the smell of. Finally, notice 1 thing you can taste or would like to taste.

This exercise works by engaging multiple sensory pathways, redirecting your attention away from emotional flooding and back to the present moment. It's particularly effective for parents who experience anxiety alongside anger, as it interrupts the spiral of catastrophic thinking that often accompanies trigger situations.

Jamie, father of an 8-year-old, describes using this technique: "When my daughter's homework meltdowns start triggering my own meltdown, I use the 5-4-3-2-1 technique. It forces me to get out of the emotional whirlpool in my head and back into my actual surroundings. By the time I get to the taste part, I'm usually calm enough to help her rather than join her in her tantrum."

Emergency Phrase Reset (5 seconds)

In the heat of a triggering moment, sometimes all you need is a brief cognitive interrupt—a thought that creates just enough space between stimulus and response to choose differently. Developing a personal mantra that reminds you of your parenting values can serve as this interrupt.

Effective emergency phrases include:

- "This is temporary."

- "I am the adult in this situation."

- "They're having a hard time, not giving me a hard time."

- "This moment will pass."

- "I choose connection over correction right now."

The key is to find a phrase that resonates deeply with your values and practice repeating it during calm moments. When a trigger situation arises, the familiar phrase will be more accessible, creating that crucial pause before reaction.

Aisha, mother of three, shares her experience: "My emergency phrase is 'This is not an emergency.' It reminds me that even though my body feels like there's a four-alarm fire when my kids are fighting or refusing to listen, these are normal parenting challenges, not true crises. It helps me respond proportionally instead of escalating."

Emergency Reset Cards: Visual Reminders When You Need Them Most

Our brains don't work well under pressure. When we're triggered, we cannot access our best thinking. This is why it's essential to have visual cues strategically placed around your home.

The concept is simple but powerful: Create small cards with your chosen reset techniques and place them in trigger hot spots throughout your living space. The refrigerator door, bathroom mirror, your car dashboard, phone lock screen, near the dinner table, and bedside drawer are all prime locations.

These visual reminders serve as external support for your prefrontal cortex when your internal resources are depleted. They work because they reduce cognitive load—you don't have to remember the techniques in the heat of the moment; you just have to follow the instructions you've left for yourself.

The cards can be as simple or creative as you like. Some parents use color coding—red for physical resets, blue for breathing techniques, green for cognitive reframes. Others include small images or symbols that trigger memory of the complete technique. The key is consistency and visibility.

Carlos, father of a teenager and a toddler, explains his system: "I have reset cards taped inside kitchen cabinets, on the back of the bathroom door, and even one laminated in the shower. They've saved me countless times when I'm about to lose it. My teenager rolled her eyes at first, but I've caught her reading them too."

Age-Specific Reset Adaptations

Resetting your nervous system looks different depending on your child's age and developmental stage. Understanding these differences helps you adapt your approach appropriately.

With Toddlers (Ages 2–4)

Toddlers exist in a perpetual state of big feelings and limited language, creating a uniquely challenging environment for parental regulation. Their developmental imperatives— exploring boundaries, asserting independence, and learning through repetition—can be particularly triggering for adults.

When you feel yourself escalating with a toddler, using exaggerated, visible breathing helps both of you calm down. Toddlers are natural mimics and will often unconsciously match your breathing pattern. Physically lowering yourself to their level reduces the intimidation factor of an angry adult looming over them while also changing your perspective, both literally and figuratively.

Sometimes, physical distance is necessary—a "mommy time-out" or "daddy reset moment." This isn't abandonment; it's modeling self-care. Explain simply: "I need to take a breath to calm my body. I'll be right back." This demonstrates that emotions require management, not suppression or explosion.

Remember that toddlers have significant developmental limitations in impulse control, emotional regulation, and language processing. Their behavior isn't personal or manipulative; it's developmentally appropriate, even when exhausting. Use simple, repetitive phrases rather than explanations: "Gentle hands" instead of a lecture on why hitting is wrong.

Mariana, mother of twin three-year-olds, shares: "I used to try reasoning with them when they were melting down, which just made all three of us more frustrated. Now, I focus on regulating myself first—big, obvious deep breaths, shoulders down, speaking slowly. It's like magic how often they'll start mimicking my calm state instead of me catching their frantic one."

With School-Age Children (Ages 5–10)

School-age children are developing greater independence, social awareness, and testing boundaries in more sophisticated ways. Their newfound verbal abilities and logical thinking skills can sometimes manifest as arguments, negotiation, or what feels like deliberate button-pushing.

When triggered by a school-age child, naming what's happening creates valuable transparency: "I'm feeling frustrated and need a moment to calm down." This labels emotions without blaming the child while modeling self-awareness. You can explicitly model the calm-down strategies you want them to use: "I'm going to count to five and take some deep breaths."

The concept of a "pause button" for heated interactions works well with this age group. Establish this as a family tool that anyone can use when emotions run high: "Let's press pause on this conversation until we're both feeling calmer."

Once everyone is regulated, engage their developing problem-solving abilities: "What could we do differently next time?" School-age children often have insightful solutions when included in the process.

Remember that what appears as "rudeness" or "disrespect" is often developmental, not personal. Children this age are learning social boundaries and testing their growing power. Responding to these tests with regulation rather than reaction teaches them how to handle their own increasing social and emotional challenges.

James, father of 7- and 9-year-old boys, notes: "When I started narrating my own regulation process out loud, my kids became fascinated. Now, they'll sometimes ask me, 'Dad, is your lid flipped?' referring to the 'lid flipping' metaphor we use for losing emotional control. It's become a family language for checking in with each other."

With Tweens and Teens (Ages 11–18)

The adolescent years bring a profound push for autonomy and identity formation that can create high-conflict situations. Hormonal changes, brain development, and social pressures create a perfect storm of emotional volatility—for them and you.

When triggered by a tween or teen, explicitly acknowledging the tension prevents escalation: "This conversation is getting heated for both of us." Normalizing the need for a reset removes shame: "Let's both take five minutes and then try again." This respects their growing maturity while maintaining boundaries.

Using "I" statements focuses on your experience rather than criticizing them: "When multiple deadlines get missed, I feel anxious and frustrated" instead of "You're so irresponsible." This approach reduces defensiveness and models emotional ownership.

Remember that the adolescent prefrontal cortex is still developing. Sometimes, their poor decisions or emotional reactions stem from brain development, not deliberate defiance. Focus on maintaining the relationship during conflicts, rather than "winning" arguments. Your connection with them is the foundation for all positive influence.

Sophia, mother of a 14-year-old, reflects: "I've learned to say, 'I need to step away so I can listen better when I come back.' This shows my daughter that my goal is understanding her, not just controlling her. It's completely changed our conflicts from power struggles to actual communication."

Modeling Self-Regulation: The Greatest Gift

When you reset in front of your children rather than away from them, you're teaching the most valuable skill they'll ever learn: emotional regulation. This doesn't mean performing calm while internally seething. It means authentically managing your emotions in real time.

The power of this modeling cannot be overstated. Children learn emotional regulation primarily through observation and experience, not through lectures or punishment. Each time you demonstrate managing your own triggers, you're creating a neural template in your child's brain for handling difficult emotions.

Try narrating your process: "I notice I'm getting frustrated. I'm going to take three deep breaths to help my body calm down. That feels better. Now we can figure this out together." This transparency demystifies emotional regulation and shows your children that emotions are manageable, not something to be afraid of.

This narration serves multiple purposes. It helps you stay conscious of your regulation process rather than going on autopilot. It gives your children language for their own emotional experiences. And it normalizes the reality that all humans—even adults—experience big feelings that require management.

Over time, you may notice your children adopting your regulation strategies. A 4-year-old taking deep breaths during a frustrating task or a teenager saying "I need a minute" before responding to an upsetting situation—these are the fruits of your modeling, more powerful than any lecture could ever be.

Mark, father of an 11-year-old with anxiety, shares: "My daughter used to have these massive meltdowns that triggered my own anxiety. I started very deliberately talking through my calming process out loud: 'My heart is racing. I'm going to put my hand on my chest and breathe slowly to help it slow down.' Now, she uses the exact same technique and language when she's anxious. She didn't learn it from a book or a therapist—she learned it from watching me."

Troubleshooting Your Reset

Even with the best intentions and techniques, you'll encounter situations where resetting feels impossible. Here's how to handle common challenges.

When You Can't Calm Down

Sometimes, triggers are too intense or arrive too rapidly for your usual techniques to work. In these moments, focus on creating physical distance if possible: "I need five minutes to cool down." This isn't a punishment or abandonment; it's a responsible recognition of your limits.

Use extreme simplicity in communication: "We'll talk when I'm calm." Complex explanations require prefrontal cortex function, which is compromised when you're highly triggered. Focus exclusively on safety until you can regulate.

If another adult is available, tag them in. This isn't failure—it's wisdom. Recognizing when you need backup is a strength, not a weakness. If you're parenting solo, remember that stepping away briefly to regulate is better than staying present in a dysregulated state.

Most importantly, remember that modeling repair after losing it is also valuable. Perfect regulation isn't the goal (or even possible). The cycle of rupture and repair builds resilience and trust when done with authenticity and responsibility.

When the Triggers Keep Coming

Parents sometimes experience what therapists call "trigger stacking," multiple triggers arriving so rapidly that you can't fully reset between them. This creates a state of chronic activation where even small incidents can cause big reactions.

When you notice this happening, drastically simplify expectations for everyone. This isn't the day for elaborate meals, complex projects, or challenging social situations. Focus only on basic needs temporarily: food, rest, safety, connection.

Reach out for support through partners, friends, or family members. Even a five-minute phone call to vent can release enough pressure to continue functioning. Send the text, make the call, ask for the help—connection is a biological need, not a luxury.

See repeated trigger stacking as a sign of your overall load, not a measure of your parenting ability. It's often a sign that your system is overtaxed in ways that require structural changes, not just better in-the-moment techniques.

When You Yell Despite Your Best Efforts

Even with all these tools, there will be times when you yell. When this happens, skip the shame spiral—it doesn't help you or your children. Shame reduces access to your prefrontal cortex, making positive change less likely, not more.

Remember that repair is part of the process, not a failure of the process. Every parent-child relationship involves ruptures. The difference between secure and insecure attachment isn't the absence of ruptures—it's the presence of consistent repair.

Use yelling incidents as information about your current capacity and triggering contexts, not as evidence of parental failure. What preceded the yelling? What resources were depleted? This information helps you prevent similar situations rather than just feeling bad about them.

Implement a simple repair (which we'll cover in Tool 8) that acknowledges impact without excessive self-flagellation. Then return to self-compassion—you're learning a new skill in extremely challenging circumstances.

The Reset Button: Your Foundation for Everything Else

The reset button isn't just the first tool in this book—it's the foundation for every other technique we'll explore. Without the ability to manage your emotional state, no parenting strategy will work consistently.

Each time you successfully interrupt the yell-regret cycle, you strengthen the neural pathways that make regulation easier the next time. You're rewiring your brain's default response to stress. This is neuroplasticity in action—the brain's remarkable ability to change in response to repeated experiences.

The goal isn't to never feel triggered—that's not realistic. The goal is to expand the space between stimulus and response, creating room to choose a different course of action.

The reset button is your way of expanding that space, one breath at a time. And in doing so, you're not just becoming the parent you want to be—you're giving your children the priceless gift of emotional regulation that will serve them throughout their lives.

In the next chapter, we'll explore how to build on this foundation with the respect loop—a powerful tool for modeling the behavior you want to see from your children. But for now, focus on strengthening your reset button. It's the most important parenting skill you'll ever develop.

Quick tip: When you feel yourself getting heated, use the 4-6-8 breath: Inhale for 4 counts, hold for 6, exhale for 8. This activates your parasympathetic nervous system, hitting the "calm" button before words you might regret can escape.

Reset Button Reflection Questions

1. What are your three most common triggers with your children?

2. Which physical sensations alert you that you're becoming triggered?

3. Which reset technique seems most accessible to you in stressful moments?

4. How might you adapt these techniques to your specific family situation?

5. What would success look like for you in terms of managing your triggers?

TOOL 2:
THE RESPECT LOOP

Do you remember being told as a child, "Respect your elders"?

For many of us, respect was presented as a one-way street—something children owed adults simply because of age. The problem? This approach creates a fundamental disconnect in our relationships with our children. We demand respect while simultaneously using disrespectful communication tactics, such as yelling, threatening, or dismissing. Then, we wonder why our kids don't "respect" us.

Let me introduce what I call the respect loop—a revolutionary yet simple concept that transforms your relationship with your children and breaks the cycle of disrespectful communication.

The Paradox of Demanded Respect

Picture this: You've asked your eight-year-old to put away their shoes three times. They continue playing as if you hadn't spoken. Frustration builds until you snap, "How many times do I have to tell you? Put your shoes away *now*! Why don't you ever listen to me?"

In that moment, you're demanding respect (*Listen when I speak*) while communicating disrespectfully (yelling, using contemptuous language, implying character flaws). This creates a paradox that your child's brain simply cannot resolve. The message becomes: "Do as I say, not as I do."

Research in developmental psychology shows that children learn primarily through observation, not instruction[6]. When we demand behaviors we don't model, we create cognitive dissonance that manifests as resistance, defiance, or shutdown—the exact opposite of what we want.

The Science of Modeling

Neuroscience gives us fascinating insights into why modeling works so powerfully. When children observe their parents, specialized brain cells called mirror neurons activate, essentially rehearsing the observed behavior in their own minds. These neurons create neural templates that become the foundation for your child's behavioral responses.

This isn't just theoretical. A 2019 study found that children whose parents modeled respectful communication had significantly higher emotional intelligence and better peer relationships than children whose parents demanded respect but used disrespectful communication tactics[7].

The implications are profound: Your children will become what you are, not what you tell them to be.

---

[6] Rymanowicz, 2015
[7] López-Martínez et al, 2019

Creating Your Respect Loop

The respect loop has three key components that work together to transform your family communication:

Model First, Expect Second

The fundamental principle is devastatingly simple: If you want respect, you must give it first. This means:

- speaking to your child in the same tone you'd use with a respected colleague or friend

- making requests rather than demands

- giving full attention when they speak to you (yes, that means putting down your phone)

- acknowledging their perspective even when you disagree

- apologizing genuinely when you make mistakes

Lisa, mother of three, describes her transformation: "I realized I was speaking to my kids in ways I would never speak to another adult. When I started treating them with the same basic courtesy I'd show a friend, their whole demeanor changed. My 10-year-old actually said, 'Mom, I like talking to you now.'"

Name and Notice Respect

Children can't develop skills they can't identify. Make respect visible by naming it explicitly:

- "I appreciate how respectfully you just expressed your disappointment."

- "I notice that when we both speak calmly, we solve problems much faster."

- "I respect your opinion on this, even though I see it differently."

You can also notice respectful communication in books, movies, or real-life interactions: "Did you notice how that cashier spoke so respectfully to the customer who was upset? She stayed calm and really listened."

This naming practice develops your child's respect radar—their ability to recognize and value respectful communication in any context.

Repair Respect Ruptures

Even with the best intentions, you'll have moments when you communicate disrespectfully. The magic isn't in perfect communication—it's in consistent repair.

Here's what to do when you've broken the respect loop:

1. Acknowledge it specifically: "I spoke to you disrespectfully when I rolled my eyes and used that sarcastic tone."

2. Take responsibility without excuses: "That wasn't the way I want to communicate with you."

3. Recommit to respect: "You deserve to be spoken to respectfully, even when I'm frustrated."

These repair moments aren't failures in the process—they're opportunities to strengthen the respect loop by demonstrating that respect is a value you hold even when you fall short of your ideal.

Miguel, father of a teenager, shares: "Our breakthrough came when I started acknowledging when I communicated disrespectfully. Instead of pretending the yelling didn't happen, I'd circle back and say, 'I didn't handle that respectfully. You deserve better.' Now my son does the same when he catches himself being disrespectful. It's like we've created this mutual accountability."

Respect Across Developmental Stages

The implementation of the respect loop shifts across different ages and stages:

With Toddlers (Ages 2–4)

For toddlers, respect looks like acknowledging their emerging autonomy while maintaining necessary boundaries. Simple strategies include the following:

- Offer limited choices to honor their growing independence: "Would you like to wear the red shirt or the blue shirt?"

- Speak in plain, direct language about expectations: "Gentle hands with the dog" rather than "How many times have I told you not to be rough?"

- Acknowledge big feelings without shaming them: "You're really angry right now. It's okay to feel angry, but it's not okay to hit."

Remember that respectful communication with toddlers isn't about treating them like miniature adults—it's about honoring their developmental stage while still providing the structure they need.

Jamal, father of twins, notes: "When I started treating my three-year-olds' preferences as valid—even small things like which cup they wanted—the power struggles decreased dramatically. They felt respected and became more cooperative overall."

With School-Age Children (Ages 5–10)

School-age children are developing social awareness and are highly attuned to fairness. For them, respect looks like this:

- Explain the reasoning behind rules and expectations: "We brush our teeth twice daily because it prevents painful cavities and expensive dental work."

- Acknowledge their growing expertise: "You know a lot about dinosaurs! Can you tell me more about why the Triceratops had that frill?"

- Involve them in family decisions at an appropriate level: "We need to figure out weekend chores. What ideas do you have for making this fair for everyone?"

This age group thrives on respect that acknowledges their growing competence while still providing the guidance they need.

Anika, mother of an eight-year-old, shares: "My breakthrough came when I stopped saying 'Because I said so.' Instead, I started explaining my reasoning. Sometimes she still disagrees, but she feels respected when I take the time to help her understand my thinking."

With Tweens and Teens (Ages 11–18)

Adolescents are exquisitely sensitive to disrespect as they form their identities. For them, respect includes these actions:

- Take their opinions seriously, even when you disagree: "I see this differently, but I appreciate you thinking this through."

- Respect appropriate privacy: Knock before entering their room, avoid reading journals or messages without permission except in safety concerns.

- Acknowledge their developing adult capabilities: "I trust your judgment on this" or "I'd like to hear what you think we should do."

With this age group, respect means treating them like the adults they are becoming while still providing the guidance they continue to need.

David, father of a 16-year-old, reflects: "The game-changer was when I started asking her opinion on real issues—politics, ethical dilemmas, family decisions. She rose to the occasion and started treating our conversations with more maturity because I signaled that I respected her thinking."

When the Loop Breaks Down

The respect loop will face challenges. Here's how to handle common scenarios:

When You're Met With Disrespect

When your respectful communication is met with eye-rolling, backtalk, or ignoring, remember this isn't a failure of the approach—it's part of the process. Children test new patterns to see if they're consistent, and they've likely developed habits of disrespectful communication that take time to unlearn.

Here's how to respond:

- Name the dynamic calmly: "I notice I'm speaking respectfully, but that comment felt disrespectful to me."

- Recommit to the loop: "I'm going to keep communicating respectfully because that's important to me."

- Set a clear boundary: "I want to continue this conversation when we can speak respectfully to each other."

The key is consistency—maintain your side of the loop even when it's not immediately reciprocated. Children need to see that your respect isn't conditional on their behavior.

When Cultural Differences Create Confusion

Families navigate diverse cultural expectations around respect, some of which may emphasize hierarchy and deference over reciprocity. If you're transitioning from a more traditional "respect your elders" paradigm to a reciprocal respect model, acknowledge this explicitly:

"In our family, we're learning a new way of showing respect to each other. This might be different from how Grandma and Grandpa expect respect, and that's okay. Different families have different respect traditions."

This transparency helps children navigate varying expectations while understanding your family values.

When Other Adults Undermine the Loop

When other caregivers or family members don't share your respect approach, focus on consistency in your own interactions rather than trying to convert everyone. You might say, "In our household, we're practicing speaking respectfully to each other, even when we're upset. It's still a work in progress, but it's important to me."

Your modeling will have the most powerful impact, even if it's not reinforced in every environment your child encounters.

The Ripple Effects of Respect

As you commit to the respect loop, you'll begin to notice changes that extend far beyond communication:

Internal Changes in Your Child

Children raised with reciprocal respect develop these essential traits:

- stronger self-regulation skills (they've observed these modeled consistently)

- higher self-esteem (they experience themselves as worthy of respect)

- better conflict resolution abilities (they've witnessed respectful disagreement)

- more authentic communication (they don't need to hide or lie to avoid disrespectful responses)

These internal developments create the foundation for lifelong emotional health.

External Changes in Relationships

The respect loop transforms your day-to-day interactions:

- decreased power struggles (respect reduces the need to assert dominance)

- more honest communication (respect creates psychological safety)

- increased cooperation (human beings naturally reciprocate respect)

- increased joy and connection (respect removes the barriers created by fear and resentment)

These relationship changes make daily family life more peaceful and connected.

Transgenerational Changes

Perhaps most powerfully, the respect loop can break intergenerational patterns:

- Your children learn a new template for all relationships.

- They're more likely to choose respectful partners and friends.

- They'll parent their own children with respect rather than fear or control.

- The patterns of respectful communication ripple outward into the world.

This is how meaningful change happens—one family at a time, one interaction at a time.

From Theory to Practice: Your Respect Loop Action Plan

Start implementing the respect loop with these concrete steps:

1. Conduct a respect audit: For one day, notice how you communicate with your children versus how you communicate with other adults. Where are the discrepancies?

2. Choose one respect upgrade: Select one common interaction that could use a respect upgrade. Perhaps it's morning routines, homework time, or bedtime. Focus on transforming just that interaction initially.

3. Create visible reminders: Post small notes in trigger spots with phrases like "Speak as if they're someone else's children" or "Model first, expect second."

4. Develop a respectful request format: Replace commands with a consistent, respectful request structure: "Would you please [specific action] by [specific time]? Thank you."

5. Practice the repair script: Rehearse your repair response for moments when you communicate disrespectfully: "I just spoke disrespectfully when I [specific behavior]. That's not how I want to communicate with you. Let me try again."

The respect loop isn't just another parenting technique—it's a fundamental shift in how we view our relationships with our children. When we move from demanded deference to mutual respect, we create the conditions for authentic connection, willing cooperation, and lifelong emotional health.

In the next chapter, we'll build on this foundation with the calm script—specific language patterns that de-escalate tension and build connection even in challenging moments.

Quick tip: Children learn respect through experiencing it, not by being commanded to show it. Before making a request, ask yourself: *Would I speak this way to a friend?* If not, adjust your tone to model the respect you want to receive.

Respect Loop Reflection Questions

1. What were the respect norms in your family growing up?

2. In what situations do you find it most challenging to communicate respectfully with your children?

3. What's one respect upgrade you could implement immediately?

4. How might your relationship with your child transform if respect truly became reciprocal?

5. What would help you remember to repair respect ruptures consistently?

Tool 3:
The Calm Script

It's bath time. Your 4-year-old is running naked through the house, giggling maniacally while you chase after them, already 30 minutes past bedtime. Your 7-year-old still has homework to finish. Your partner is working late. And you've just stepped on a LEGO brick with your bare foot.

What comes out of your mouth in this moment?

For most of us, it's some version of "EVERYONE NEEDS TO LISTEN RIGHT NOW OR THERE WILL BE CONSEQUENCES!" delivered at a volume that makes the dog hide under the couch.

But what if you had another option? Not a script that requires superhuman patience or acting skills, but a practical, accessible way to communicate effectively even when you're at your limit?

That's exactly what the calm script provides—language patterns that work even when you don't feel calm, that connect rather than alienate, and that increase cooperation rather than compliance.

Why Traditional Scripts Fail

Before we dive into the calm script, let's understand why common communication approaches often backfire:

- **The threat script**: "If you don't put those toys away right now, I'm throwing them all in the trash!" This creates short-term compliance through fear but damages trust and teaches manipulation rather than responsibility.

- **The guilt script**: "After everything I do for you, you can't even pick up your room?" This creates shame, which research consistently shows leads to either rebellion or unhealthy compliance based on fear of rejection[8]. Neither builds the internal motivation we want our children to develop.

- **The logic overload script**: "You need to get ready for bed now because if you don't get enough sleep, your brain won't consolidate memories properly and you'll have trouble with your test tomorrow, plus sleep deprivation impacts immune function and..." This overwhelms children's cognitive processing (especially when they are already tired or emotional) and overlooks the emotional component of resistance, which is rarely about a lack of information.

- **The inconsistency script**: Toggling unpredictably between gentle requests and explosive demands confuses children's developing nervous systems and

---

[8] Veldhuis et al., 2014

creates anxiety as they can't predict what response their behavior will elicit.

If these scripts sound familiar, you're not alone. Most of us default to the communication patterns we experienced as children or resort to whatever seems most likely to generate immediate compliance when we're stressed.

The calm script offers a better way.

The Neuroscience of Calm Communication

When you communicate calmly—even when you don't feel calm on the inside—you create a neurobiological environment that is conducive to cooperation and learning.

When children hear yelling or threats, their amygdala activates, triggering stress responses that shut down the prefrontal cortex's essential functions for listening, reasoning, and self-regulation. Essentially, you can't reason with a brain in survival mode.

In contrast, calm communication helps co-regulate your child's nervous system. Your steady voice and measured breathing patterns help stabilize their physiological state through a process neuroscientists call "interpersonal neurobiology." Their brain synchronizes with yours.

This synchronization isn't just theoretical—it has been observed in laboratory settings, where parent-child brain waves align during calm, connected interactions[9]. This state of

---

[9] Bennet et al., 2015

"neural resonance" creates the optimal conditions for both cooperation and learning.

The Four Elements of The Calm Script

The calm script consists of four key elements that work together to transform communication even in challenging moments. The beauty of this approach is that it doesn't require you to be perfectly calm inside—just to communicate in ways that foster connection and cooperation.

The Connect-Before-Correct Opener

The first crucial seconds of communication set the tone for everything that follows. Rather than leading with demands or corrections, the calm script begins with a brief connection:

1. Use their name warmly: "Emma..."

2. Acknowledge their current state/activity: "I see you're really enjoying that game..."

3. Make a brief physical connection when appropriate: Try a gentle hand on the shoulder or sitting beside them.

4. Match their eye level: Kneel or sit to speak with younger children.

This opener takes just seconds but dramatically increases receptivity to what follows. It signals safety rather than threat, shifting their brain from a defensive posture to a receptive mode.

Marco, father of a five-year-old, shares: "Starting with 'Luca, I notice you're working hard on that drawing' instead of 'Put that down, it's dinner time' completely changed his responsiveness. That three-second connection prevents five minutes of power struggle."

The Clear, Concise Request

After connection comes clarity. The most effective requests are:

- Specific and behavioral: "Please put your shoes in the basket" rather than "Clean up your mess."

- Positively framed: "Walk in the house" rather than "Don't run."

- Brief: Use 10 words or fewer for the core request.

- Singular: Give one request at a time rather than a series.

- Straightforward: Steer clear of lecturing, history, or unnecessary explanation.

This clarity serves both you and your child. It prevents the cognitive overwhelm that comes with long explanations, particularly when a child is already emotionally activated or tired. It also helps you distill exactly what you need, separating essential requests from those that are preference-based.

Leila, mother of twins, notes: "I realized I was giving my six-year-olds five-part instructions and then getting frustrated when they only did one part. Now I make one clear request, wait for completion, then make the next. It seems like it would take longer, but we actually get through routines faster with less frustration."

The Validation Bridge

When children resist requests (which they inevitably will), the calm script includes validating their feelings before restating expectations. This validation does all of the following:

- It acknowledges emotions without judgment: "You're disappointed about stopping your game."

- It normalizes feelings while maintaining boundaries: "It's natural to feel frustrated AND we need to get ready for bed."

- It creates psychological space for processing: "I understand AND we still need to..."

This validation isn't just being nice—it's a neurologically sound strategy. When emotions are acknowledged, the limbic system calms, allowing the prefrontal cortex to come back online for reasoning and cooperation.

Sasha, father of a strong-willed four-year-old, shares: "The word '*and*' has transformed our power struggles. Instead of arguing against her feelings, I say, 'I hear you don't want to leave the playground *and* it's time to go.' Something about that '*and*' instead of '*but*' helps her feel heard while still understanding the limit."

The Follow-Through Formula

The final component addresses what happens when requests aren't met despite connection, clarity, and validation. Rather than escalating to threats or punishments, the calm script uses calm follow-through:

- Restate the expectation once: "Jordan, the LEGO pieces need to be in the bin before screen time."

- Present a clear choice: "You can put them away now, or we can do it together, but we need to finish before the show starts."

- Follow through with matter-of-fact action rather than a punitive tone: "I see you're having trouble getting started. I'll help you with the first part."

This approach maintains your boundary while providing support rather than punishment. It focuses on solving the problem together rather than creating adversarial power struggles.

James, father of three, reflects: "I used to make huge threats when my kids didn't listen—'No electronics for a week!'—that I couldn't realistically enforce. Now, I focus on natural consequences with calm follow-through. The consistency actually works better than the big threats ever did."

Adapting the Calm Script Across Ages

The framework remains consistent, but implementation shifts across developmental stages:

For Toddlers and Preschoolers (Ages 2–5)

With young children, simplicity is key:

- Keep requests to five words or less when possible.

- Use concrete language without idioms or abstractions.

- Incorporate playfulness when appropriate: "Let's see if these blocks can jump into their home!"

- Provide physical guidance alongside verbal requests.

- Use visual supports for routine expectations.

Remember that young children are concrete thinkers with limited impulse control. Their resistance isn't defiance—it's a natural part of development. The Calm Script acknowledges these limitations while gently scaffolding developing skills.

Maya, mother of a three-year-old, explains: "Instead of repeatedly asking my daughter to get ready, I take a picture of each step (shoes on, coat on, backpack ready) and let her move through the visual sequence. The calm visual support works better than my escalating verbal requests ever did."

For Elementary-Age Children (Ages 6–10)

School-age children benefit from the following:

- Brief explanations after the clear request: "Shoes go in the basket so no one trips over them."

- Problem-solving involvement: "What would help you remember to hang up your coat?"

- Authentic choices within boundaries: "Homework can happen before or after snack—you decide which works better for you."

- Calm Scripts that acknowledge growing autonomy: "You know what you need to do to get ready for bed. Which part would you like to start with?"

This age group responds well to matter-of-fact, non-emotional communication that respects their growing capabilities while maintaining necessary structure.

Darius, father of an eight-year-old, shares: "My son responds completely differently when I say, 'Teeth need brushing before stories' in a neutral tone versus when I say, 'How many times do I have to tell you to brush your teeth?!' with frustration. The first approach invites cooperation; the second invites resistance."

For Tweens and Teens (Ages 11–18)

Adolescents need calm scripts that:

- Respect their autonomy: "What's your plan for getting your project finished on time?"

- Acknowledge their perspective: "I can see why you'd want to go to this party."

- Focus on problem-solving: "What ideas do you have for how we could work this out?"

- Provide honest information about impacts: "When the kitchen is left messy, it makes the morning rush much more stressful for everyone."

- Allow for appropriate negotiation: "I hear you want a later curfew. Let's talk about what that could look like."

With this age group, the script acknowledges their developmental need for independence while maintaining appropriate boundaries.

Elena, mother of a 14-year-old, notes: "When I shifted from lectures to calm, brief statements of expectation with my daughter, our relationship improved dramatically. She needs to know I respect her enough to be straightforward rather than manipulative or emotional in my requests."

Common Obstacles and Solutions

The calm script will face challenges in real-life implementation. Here's how to navigate common obstacles:

When You Don't Feel Remotely Calm

The beauty of the calm script is that it doesn't require you to actually feel calm—it's about communicating in a way that promotes calm. On the most difficult days:

- Focus on physical cues: Lower your voice, slow your speech, and relax your facial muscles.

- Use the shortest possible version of the script: Name + Brief Request.

- Remember that calm communication is most important precisely when you feel least calm.

Think of the calm script as an external structure that can support you when your internal resources are depleted. The script itself becomes a form of scaffolding for both you and your child.

When Time Pressure Creates Urgency

In genuine rush situations:

- Acknowledge the time pressure: "We're running late and that feels stressful."

- Use clear priority language: "Right now, shoes on is the only task that matters."

- Offer concrete help: "I'll hold your coat while you put on your shoes."

- Save fuller explanations for calmer moments: "We'll talk more about morning routines when we're not rushing."

Note the difference between actual emergencies (which are rare) and habitual rushing (which can be addressed through routine adjustments). Reserve urgency language for true urgency situations.

When Multiple Children Create Chaos

With sibling groups:

- Address children individually rather than as a collective: "Emma, please put your shoes away. Jackson, please hang up your coat."

- Use the environment rather than your voice to regain attention: Flick lights off and on, use a gentle chime.

- Establish response rituals: "When I say, 'listening ears,' you say, 'ready to hear' and freeze."

- Speak less, demonstrate more: Physically move to each child at their level for important requests.

Remember that a personalized, brief connection is more effective than general, loud announcements, even though the latter may seem more efficient in the moment.

When the Script Doesn't Work Immediately

New communication patterns take time to establish:

- Expect an adjustment period of at least three weeks.

- Notice small improvements rather than expecting perfection.

- Remember that consistency matters more than intensity.

- Acknowledge that new patterns feel awkward at first.

The shift to the calm script is more than behavioral—it's neurological. You're creating new neural pathways for communication. This process requires repetition and persistence.

From Script to Authentic Communication

The ultimate goal isn't to mechanically follow a script forever, but to internalize these communication principles until they become your natural pattern. Over time, the calm script elements become integrated into your authentic communication style.

Parents who have used this approach for months or years report that it eventually feels strange to communicate any other way. The script becomes not just what you say, but how you think about communication with your children.

As you practice, pay attention to what elements of the script feel most natural to you and which require more conscious effort. Some parents find the connection piece comes easily, while clear requests feel challenging. Others naturally state clear expectations but struggle with the validation bridge. This self-awareness helps you focus your practice where it's most needed.

Remember that perfect implementation isn't the goal—progress is. Each time you use elements of the calm script instead of defaulting to less effective patterns, you're strengthening new neural pathways and creating more positive communication cycles.

Frank, father of three, reflects after six months of practice: "It doesn't feel like a script anymore. It's just how we talk to each other now. My kids have even started using similar patterns with each other—connecting before making requests, validating feelings before stating their needs. It's like we've developed a new family language."

Calm Communication as Family Culture

As the calm script becomes your default, you'll notice a broader shift in family communication culture. Children begin mirroring these patterns back to you and using them with siblings. The emotional climate of your home gradually transforms.

This cultural shift is perhaps the most powerful outcome—beyond specific interactions, you're establishing a family environment where people feel heard, respected, and capable of working through challenges together.

The calm script isn't just a parenting technique; it's the foundation for lifelong communication skills your children will carry into future relationships. Every time you connect before correcting, validate before redirecting, or maintain calm during conflict, you're teaching your children how to do the same.

In the next chapter, we'll explore The Boundary Builder—how to establish and maintain loving limits that provide the security children need to thrive.

Quick tip: Connect before correcting. Start with "I see you're enjoying..." before making a request. This brief connection increases cooperation dramatically, turning potential power struggles into moments of working together.

Calm Script Reflection Questions

1. Which communication patterns from your own childhood do you find yourself repeating?

2. In what situations do you find it most difficult to maintain calm communication?

3. Which element of the calm script seems most challenging for you?

4. What would help you remember to use the calm script in heated moments?

5. How might your family dynamics shift if calm communication became your default?

Tool 4:
The Boundary Builder

You're driving down a mountain road with steep cliffs on either side. Would you feel safer with or without guardrails?

For most of us, the answer is obvious—guardrails create safety and freedom. When solid boundaries exist, we can enjoy the journey without constant vigilance and fear. We can look at the beautiful views instead of white-knuckling the steering wheel.

The same principle applies to children and boundaries. Far from restricting freedom, well-crafted boundaries create the secure conditions that allow children to explore, grow, and thrive. Boundaries aren't walls—they're guardrails that define the safe space within which true freedom can flourish.

Yet for many parents, setting and maintaining boundaries feels overwhelming, guilt-inducing, or triggers resistance that leads to either harsh enforcement or inconsistent surrender. The boundary builder tool transforms this dynamic, creating boundaries that provide security without rigidity, limits that convey love rather than control.

The Science of Secure Boundaries

Research in developmental psychology by the National Collaborating Centre for Mental Health (UK) in 2015 shows that children raised with clear, consistent boundaries demonstrate the following:

- better emotional regulation abilities

- higher levels of resilience

- stronger executive function skills

- more secure attachment to caregivers

- greater social competence with peers

Neurobiologically, boundaries help develop the prefrontal cortex—the brain region responsible for impulse control, planning, and emotional regulation. When children experience appropriate limits with supportive guidance, they build the neural architecture needed for self-regulation.

Dr. Dan Siegel[10], clinical professor of psychiatry, explains: "Boundaries in childhood are like banks to a river. Without them, children flood with overwhelming emotions. With boundaries that are too rigid, they're constricted and can't flow naturally. The ideal is boundaries that contain while allowing movement and growth."

This balanced approach creates what psychologists call the "authoritative parenting" sweet spot—high warmth combined

---

[10] Siegel, 2021

with clear expectations—consistently associated with the best outcomes across diverse cultures and contexts.

The Four Elements of Effective Boundaries

The boundary builder consists of four key elements that work together to create boundaries children can understand, respect, and eventually internalize:

The Clarity Foundation

Effective boundaries start with absolute clarity—for you and your child. This means:

- Identifying your non-negotiable values-based boundaries: Safety, respect, and health needs typically fall here.

- Distinguishing these from preference-based boundaries that have more flexibility: "We don't negotiate about wearing seatbelts, but you can choose which jacket to wear when it's cold."

- Articulating boundaries in specific, behavioral terms: "Feet on the floor, not on the furniture," rather than "Don't be destructive."

- Using concrete, positive language: "Food stays in the kitchen," rather than "Don't eat in the living room."

This clarity prevents the boundary drift that occurs when limits are vague or inconsistently defined. It also helps children understand exactly what is expected, reducing the confusion that often underlies resistance.

Amara, mother of three, shares: "I realized many of our conflicts stemmed from poorly defined boundaries. When I got really clear about what mattered (safety and respect) versus preferences (tidiness levels), conflicts decreased dramatically. My children weren't trying to break boundaries—they just couldn't consistently identify them."

The Connection Before Correction Sequence

The order of operations matters immensely when establishing boundaries. Here's the sequence that builds cooperation rather than resistance:

1. Connect emotionally before stating the boundary.

2. Acknowledge the child's perspective or desire.

3. State the boundary clearly and simply.

4. Offer an acceptable alternative when possible.

This might sound like: "I see you're excited about bouncing that ball [connection]. It looks really fun [perspective]. Balls need to stay outside or in the basement [boundary]. You can bounce it there or choose an inside toy instead [alternative]."

This sequence honors both the relationship and the boundary, allowing them to coexist rather than conflict. The connection creates the relational safety that makes the boundary more acceptable.

Malik, father of two, notes: "I used to lead with the boundary— 'Stop throwing that!'—which created immediate resistance. Now, I connect first: 'You've got so much energy right now!

Throwing needs to happen outside.' That brief connection completely changes how they receive the limit."

The Consistency Commitment

Perhaps the most challenging aspect of boundaries is consistency—maintaining the same limits over time, across different environments, and in various emotional states. This consistency does the following:

- creates predictability that helps children feel secure

- reduces boundary-testing behaviors

- minimizes the emotional friction of case-by-case negotiations

This doesn't mean rigid inflexibility. It means that core boundaries remain consistent while allowing appropriate flexibility for development, special circumstances, and the evolution of family needs.

The key is distinguishing between intentional flexibility ("It's a special occasion, so we're extending bedtime") and inconsistency driven by parental fatigue, guilt, or conflict avoidance ("I'm too tired to enforce bedtime tonight").

Carlos, father of a six-year-old, reflects: "My consistency breakthrough came when I realized my daughter wasn't trying to manipulate me with endless negotiations—she was logically testing whether the boundary was real. Once I maintained the same limits regardless of her reaction, the constant testing actually decreased."

The Boundary Ecosystem Approach

Rather than viewing boundaries as isolated rules, the boundary builder approaches them as an interconnected ecosystem that creates the family culture. This means:

- ensuring boundaries serve shared family values

- involving children in boundary development when developmentally appropriate

- regularly reviewing and evolving boundaries as children grow

- considering how boundaries interact with each other and with family routines

This ecological approach helps boundaries function as a coherent system rather than a collection of arbitrary rules. It also helps children understand the "why" behind limits, increasing buy-in and eventual internalization.

Sophia, mother of three ranging from four to twelve, explains: "When we started approaching boundaries as our family's ecosystem rather than Mom and Dad's rules, something shifted. Our older kids became partners in maintaining boundaries with the younger ones because they understood how the boundaries created the home environment we all valued."

Developmentally Appropriate Boundaries

Effective boundaries evolve with your child's developmental capabilities and needs:

For Toddlers and Preschoolers (Ages 2–4)

At this stage, boundaries need to be:

- Few in number: Focus on safety and essential social norms.

- Extremely concrete and specific: "Gentle touches with pets" rather than "Be respectful to animals."

- Simple: Enforce consistently with minimal verbal explanation.

- Supported by environmental design: This includes safety locks, limited choices, and physical proximity.

- Redirected rather than negotiated: "Crayons are for paper, not walls. Here's your paper."

Toddlers and preschoolers are concrete thinkers who test boundaries as a natural part of their development, not as a personal defiance. They require immediate and consistent responses to boundary crossings, without complex explanations or emotional reactions.

Kendra, mother of a two-year-old, shares: "I realized my son wasn't being 'bad' when he kept touching the TV—he was conducting a science experiment: 'What happens when I touch this?' When I stopped taking it personally and just consistently redirected him, the behavior diminished naturally."

For School-Age Children (Ages 5–10)

As cognitive abilities develop, boundaries can include:

- Gradually increased involvement in boundary-setting: "What do you think would be a fair screen time limit?"

- Gradually increased involvement in boundary-setting: "What do you think would be a fair screen time limit?"

- Natural consequences connected to the boundary: "When toys aren't put away, they're harder to find the next day."

- Growth in self-monitoring capacities: "You're learning to manage your own voice volume."

- Early foundations of values-based reasoning: "In our family, we speak respectfully to each other."

This age group thrives with boundaries that acknowledge their growing capabilities while still providing clear structure and consistent enforcement.

Omar, father of seven- and nine-year-old siblings, notes: "The game-changer was when we started having monthly family meetings to revisit and adjust boundaries together. My kids actually suggested stricter screen time limits than I would have imposed because they recognized how it affected their mood."

For Tweens and Teens (Ages 11–18)

Adolescents need boundaries that:

- shift gradually from external control to internal principles

- acknowledge their need for autonomy and identity formation

- focus on safety and values while allowing increased personal choice

- include meaningful participation in boundary development

- feature transparent reasoning ("Here's why this matters to me...")

- allow negotiation within core value parameters

This age group needs boundaries that respect their growing independence while still providing the security of clear expectations in essential areas.

Juanita, mother of a 16-year-old, reflects: "The boundaries that work now are the ones where I've clearly explained my concerns and then collaborated on solutions. When my daughter helped create the boundary, she became invested in maintaining it rather than fighting against it."

When Boundaries Meet Resistance

Every effective boundary will be tested. Here's how to navigate common challenges when applying these research-backed techniques:

When Emotions Run High

Boundary enforcement often triggers big feelings—in children and parents. Here's what to do when emotions escalate:

1. Leave room for feelings: Remember that emotional reactions don't invalidate the boundary.

2. Use brief validation: "I see you're really disappointed."

3. Maintain the boundary without escalating: "The answer is still no."

4. Offer processing support: "We can talk more about your feelings after."

5. Separate soothing from boundary changes: Comfort without compromising.

Many parents confuse emotional support with being too flexible with boundaries. You can acknowledge feelings while maintaining limits. In fact, this combination helps children develop emotional resilience—they learn that difficult feelings are survivable and don't necessarily change external realities.

Ashley, mother of a strong-willed six-year-old, shares: "I used to cave when my daughter cried about boundaries because I couldn't stand her distress. I finally realized I was teaching her that emotional displays change the rules. Now, I validate her feelings while keeping the boundary firm. She still gets upset sometimes, but recovers much faster."

When Testing Is Relentless

Some children test boundaries with extraordinary persistence. When this occurs, do this:

1. Recognize that intense testing often indicates a need for more consistency, not less.

2. Use fewer words and more action as testing continues.

3. Implement matter-of-fact consequences without emotional escalation.

4. Avoid getting pulled into power struggles or negotiations during active testing.

5. Remember that consistent boundaries eventually reduce testing, even if it temporarily increases.

The children who test most persistently are often those who need the security of consistent boundaries the most. Their testing is a form of unconscious verification: "Can I trust this limit to remain stable?"

Michael, father of a boundary-testing four-year-old, reflects: "My breakthrough came when I realized my son wasn't trying to drive me crazy—he was checking if I meant what I said. When I stayed steady through multiple tests without getting emotional, he actually became more relaxed. He needed to know the boundary was solid."

When Co-Parents Disagree

Boundary inconsistency between caregivers creates confusion and increases testing. When boundaries differ between adults, try this:

1. Address discrepancies privately, not in front of children.

2. Focus on underlying values rather than specific rules.

3. Seek compromise boundaries that both parents can consistently enforce.

4. Distinguish between core safety/values boundaries and preference-based boundaries.

5. Accept that different contexts (homes, caregivers) may have somewhat different boundaries.

While perfect consistency across all caregivers isn't realistic, alignment on core boundaries provides necessary security for children.

Lin, co-parenting with her ex-husband, explains: "We have different standards for screen time in our homes, which initially created chaos during transitions. Instead of fighting about it, we agreed on basic safety boundaries that remain consistent, and we're transparent with our daughter that 'Dad's house and Mom's house have different screen rules.' The clear expectation at each location actually reduced her anxiety."

Common Boundary Pitfalls

Even well-intentioned parents encounter challenges in building effective boundaries. Here are the most common traps:

The Empty Threat Trap

When you state consequences you don't enforce: "If you do that one more time, we're leaving the party!" (but you never actually leave). This teaches that your boundaries are negotiable and your words unreliable.

Instead: Only state consequences you're willing and able to implement consistently. Start with small, manageable consequences before escalating to larger ones.

Sarah, mother of twins, shares: "I used to make huge threats in moments of frustration—'No TV for a month!'—that I couldn't possibly maintain. My kids learned to wait out my anger because they knew the boundary would dissolve. Now I stick to realistic consequences I can enforce every time: 'If you continue to argue about the game, the iPad goes away for the rest of today.' They know I mean exactly what I say."

The Inconsistency Spiral

When boundaries shift based on your energy level, public setting, or the intensity of your child's reaction. This pattern creates a constant negotiation environment where children logically invest in testing and pushing.

Instead: Identify your core non-negotiable boundaries and maintain them consistently regardless of circumstance, while being transparent about areas with flexibility.

Diego, father of a five-year-old, notes: "I realized my daughter's tantrums were worse in public because my boundaries got wobbly when I felt embarrassed. When I committed to maintaining the same limits regardless of location, her testing decreased everywhere."

The Relationship Rupture Fear

When you avoid boundaries due to worry that limits will damage connection or that your child will feel unloved. This creates insecurity as children sense the unstable foundation.

Instead: Recognize that healthy boundaries strengthen attachment by creating the predictable security children need. Connection can remain strong within clear limits.

Mia, mother of a sensitive eight-year-old, reflects: "I worried that firm boundaries would hurt our close relationship. What I discovered was the opposite—when I got clearer about limits, my son became more secure and our connection deepened. He needed the security of knowing where the lines were."

The Explanation Overload

When you attempt to secure cooperation through extensive reasoning rather than clear, consistent boundaries. This creates cognitive overwhelm and teaches children to engage in debates rather than respect limits.

Instead: Provide brief, age-appropriate explanations a single time, then move to consistent enforcement without repeated justifications. The boundary itself becomes the teacher.

Robert, father of three, shares: "I used to think if I just explained thoroughly enough why hitting wasn't okay, my three-year-old would stop. I'd give dissertations on empathy while he zoned out. When I switched to a simple 'We don't hit. Hitting hurts,' followed by consistent consequences, the behavior improved dramatically."

From Boundaries to Values

The ultimate purpose of boundaries isn't restriction but liberation. Effective boundaries gradually shift from external limits to internalized values.

In early childhood, boundaries are primarily enforced externally: "We don't hit" with physical intervention as needed. As children develop, boundaries become increasingly verbal: "Remember, hands are for helping, not hurting." Eventually, boundaries transform into internalized values: "I want to treat others with kindness."

This evolution doesn't happen automatically. It requires the following:

- Explicit connection between boundaries and underlying values: "We speak respectfully in our family because everyone deserves to feel valued."

- Gradual transfer of monitoring from parent to child: "You're learning to manage your own media choices."

- Recognition and reinforcement of internally-motivated choices: "You chose to share even though you weren't required to."

- Ongoing conversations about the principles behind family boundaries: "Why do you think this matters to us?"

This developmental progression turns boundaries from something that constrains children into something that empowers them—the capacity for principled self-regulation based on internalized values.

Elena, mother of children aged 8 and 14, observes: "With my teenager, I've watched boundaries evolve from externally enforced rules to internally-held values. Recently, she declined an invitation to a party she knew would include activities that violated her own principles—not because she feared consequences from me, but because the boundary had become her own. That's the whole point of the journey."

Building Your Family's Boundary System

Start implementing the boundary builder with these practical steps:

Conduct a Boundary Audit

Assess your current boundary landscape:

- Which boundaries do you maintain consistently?

- Which boundaries tend to drift or collapse under pressure?

- Where do you see the most boundary testing from your children?

- Which boundaries trigger the most emotional reactions in you?

This self-assessment provides a realistic starting point for improvement.

Clarify Your Non-Negotiables

Identify 3–5 core boundaries that align with your deepest family values. These might include:

- physical and emotional safety boundaries

- health and well-being boundaries

- respect and communication boundaries

- core moral or ethical boundaries

Being crystal clear about your non-negotiables helps you invest your consistency energy where it matters most.

Create a Visual Boundary Map

For younger children, a visual representation of key boundaries creates clarity:

- Use simple images for behavioral expectations.

- Post routines with clear boundaries (morning, bedtime, etc.).

- Create a family values poster connecting boundaries to principles.

- Include both the boundary and the acceptable alternatives.

This visual support reduces verbal repetition and helps children internalize expectations.

Establish Boundary Language

Develop consistent, clear language for boundaries in your family:

- Choose positive phrasing: "Feet on the floor" vs. "Don't stand on the couch."

- Create memorable boundary phrases: "Kind words, kind hands."

- Distinguish between safety boundaries and preference boundaries: "That's a safety rule" vs. "That's my preference."

- Develop standard responses to testing: "The boundary hasn't changed."

Consistent language creates a shared family understanding of expectations.

Practice the Enforce-Connect-Teach Cycle

When boundaries are tested, follow this sequence:

1. Enforce the boundary calmly and consistently.

2. Connect with empathy for any resulting disappointment.

3. Teach appropriate alternatives or skills for next time.

This cycle maintains necessary limits while preserving relationship and building future capabilities.

The boundary builder isn't about controlling children through fear or punishment. It's about creating a secure, predictable environment within which children can safely grow toward autonomy. When implemented with consistency and connection, boundaries become not a source of restriction but a foundation for true freedom.

In the next chapter, we'll explore the conversation catcher— how to create open communication channels that allow children to share their authentic thoughts and feelings, even about difficult topics.

Quick tip: Frame boundaries positively in specific, behavioral terms: "Feet on the floor" rather than "Don't stand on the couch." Clear, consistent boundaries create the secure conditions that allow true freedom to flourish.

Boundary Builder Reflection Questions

1. Which boundaries feel clearest in your family, and which tend to drift?

2. How were boundaries handled in your childhood, and how does that influence your approach now?

3. What's the difference between a boundary that creates security and one that creates resentment?

4. Which boundary challenges seem most persistent with your children?

5. How might clearer boundaries actually increase freedom in your family?

Tool 5:
The Conversation Catcher

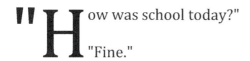"How was school today?" "Fine."

"What did you learn?"

"Nothing."

"Did anything interesting happen?"

"No."

Sound familiar? This conversational dead-end frustrates parents everywhere. We genuinely want to know about our children's inner worlds—their thoughts, feelings, experiences, and challenges. Yet so often, our attempts at connection are met with one-word answers, shrugs, or the dreaded eye roll.

What if there were a better way to invite meaningful conversation? A way that made your children want to share their thoughts and experiences with you? That's exactly what the conversation catcher provides—a framework for creating the conditions where authentic communication can flourish.

The Science of Open Communication

The more we directly push children to communicate, the more they tend to withdraw. But when we create the right conditions, meaningful sharing happens naturally and abundantly.

This pattern has neurobiological roots. Direct questioning activates the brain's threat-detection system, particularly in children who are tired, stressed, or developmentally primed for increasing privacy (hello, adolescence). In contrast, creating a secure conversational environment activates the brain's affiliation and reward systems, making sharing feel good rather than threatening.

Dr. Laurence Steinberg[11], a leading adolescent development researcher, explains: "The parent-child relationship functions best as a secure base from which the child can explore independence, not as an interrogation room. When teenagers perceive conversations as voluntary rather than coerced, their willingness to share increases dramatically."

This principle applies across all stages of development. From toddlers to teens, children share most readily when they feel safe, respected, and in control of their narrative.

The Five Elements of the Conversation Catcher

The conversation catcher consists of five key elements that work together to create an environment where meaningful communication can thrive. Think of these as building the conversational equivalent of a beautiful, open field rather than

---

[11] Singer, 2014

a tight corner—a space where your child has room to run with their thoughts rather than feeling trapped by your expectations.

The Side-By-Side Setting

The physical context of conversation profoundly impacts openness. The most effective sharing often happens:

- During parallel activities rather than face-to-face interrogations: driving in the car, walking the dog, preparing dinner, working on projects side-by-side

- In neutral territory rather than charged settings: not during discipline moments or when you're visibly frustrated

- During transition times: the 20 minutes before sleep, right after school, before starting homework, during commutes

- In environments with a physical "third thing" to focus on: nature walks, building something together, shooting baskets

This side-by-side positioning reduces the intensity of direct eye contact, which many children, especially those who are anxious, neurodivergent, or going through typical developmental phases of increased privacy, find overwhelming for sensitive conversations.

Maria, mother of a 12-year-old, shares: "My breakthrough came when I stopped trying to have heart-to-hearts sitting across from my daughter at the kitchen table. Now, our deepest conversations happen while baking cookies together or during our evening dog walk. Something about the casual side-by-side positioning makes sharing feel less intense for her."

The Non-Urgent Approach

Timing shapes willingness to engage. The most productive conversations happen when:

- You signal openness without demanding immediate response.

- The conversation feels like an invitation rather than an obligation.

- There's no pressure to reach a particular conclusion quickly.

- The child controls the depth and pacing of sharing.

- Multiple brief exchanges build over time rather than one exhaustive discussion.

This non-urgent approach creates psychological safety that makes vulnerability possible. It respects children's need to process at their own pace rather than performing connection on our schedule.

Raj, father of twin eight-year-olds, notes: "I used to fire questions the moment they got in the car after school, expecting immediate debriefs about their day. Now, I start with 'I'm here whenever you want to talk' and then we just drive quietly or listen to music. It's amazing how much more they share when they don't feel rushed or interrogated."

The Curiosity Stance

The quality of your attention dramatically impacts children's willingness to share. The conversation catcher uses a stance of genuine curiosity, characterized by the following:

- Use open-ended questions that invite elaboration: "What was that like for you?" rather than "Did you have fun?"

- Give minimal encouraging responses that show interest without taking over: "Really?" "Hmm," "Tell me more about that."

- Follow the child's conversational lead rather than redirecting to your concerns. For example, when your child starts discussing a video game character, but you're curious about their math test, stay with the game discussion rather than changing the subject.

- Comfort with silence and pauses rather than filling every gap. For instance, waiting patiently for 5-10 seconds after asking a thoughtful question, allowing the child time to gather their thoughts instead of rephrasing or answering for them.

- Withhold immediate judgment, advice, or problem-solving. Such as responding to "I got in an argument with Alex today" with "I'm listening" rather than immediately saying "Well, you should apologize" or "That's what happens when you're not patient."

This curiosity stance signals that you're interested in understanding their experience rather than seeking specific information or steering toward predetermined conclusions.

Tamika, mother of a quiet six-year-old, shares: "I realized I was shutting down conversations by jumping in with advice after his first sentence. When I shifted to just being curious—'What happened next?' or 'How did you feel about that?'—he started telling these amazing detailed stories I'd never heard before."

The Emotional Safety Container

Children share authentically only when they feel emotionally safe. This safety container includes:

- responding calmly to unexpected or difficult information

- separating your emotional reactions from the conversation itself

- validating feelings even when you disagree with behaviors or conclusions

- avoiding punishment or lectures for what's shared honestly

- respecting appropriate privacy and confidentiality

This emotional safety becomes the foundation for increasingly meaningful exchanges. When children learn that sharing doesn't lead to judgment, lecture, or emotional fallout, their openness naturally expands.

Jackson, father of a teenager, reflects: "The turning point in our relationship was when my son shared something difficult and I just listened without freaking out. He tested me with something small, and when I stayed calm, he gradually started sharing bigger things. It's like he needed to verify the emotional container could hold harder conversations."

The Narrative Invitation

The specific language you use can either open or close a conversation. Here are the most effective invitations:

- Use story prompts rather than fact-finding questions: "Tell me about a moment that made you smile today" rather than "How was your day?"

- Offer conversation starters without demanding responses: "I noticed you seemed quiet after the game. I'm here if you want to talk about it."

- Share your own relevant experiences briefly without dominating: "That reminds me of when I was nervous about my first recital. I remember feeling..."

- Provide multiple entry points through different question types: "What was challenging? What was interesting? What surprised you?"

- Normalize struggle and imperfection: "Did anything go differently than you expected today?"

These narrative invitations create doorways your child can choose to walk through rather than conversational traps they need to escape.

Elise, mother of three, explains: "I completely transformed our dinner conversations by switching from 'How was school?' to 'What made you laugh today?' or 'Tell us about something that confused you.' Suddenly, everyone was sharing these rich, specific moments instead of just saying 'fine.'"

Adapting Across Developmental Stages

The conversation catcher framework remains consistent across ages, but implementation shifts with development:

For Toddlers and Preschoolers (Ages 2–5)

Young children's communication thrives with:

- Concrete rather than abstract prompts: "Tell me about this drawing" rather than "How are you feeling?"

- Play-based communication: using toys, puppets, or pretend scenarios to express thoughts indirectly

- Physical proximity paired with conversational invitations: snuggling while asking, "What should we talk about?"

- Sensory engagement alongside verbal exchange: drawing, building, or moving while talking

- Simple emotion labeling: "You look excited! Did something fun happen?"

Remember that young children often process experiences through play rather than direct discussion. Creating space for this play becomes a form of conversation catching.

Lucia, mother of a three-year-old, shares: "My daughter rarely answers direct questions about her day at preschool. But if I set up her dolls after school and say, 'I wonder what Baby Doll did today?' she'll immediately launch into a detailed narrative about everything that happened—just projected onto the doll instead of telling it directly."

For Elementary-Age Children (Ages 6–10)

School-age children respond well to:

- Activity-based conversation: talking while building LEGO, baking, or shooting hoops

- Quality time: regular special time with each parent where conversation can unfold naturally

- Rose/thorn/bud format: something good, something challenging, something they're looking forward to

- Structured sharing rituals: highs and lows at dinner, gratitude moments at bedtime

- Indirect communication through books or media: "That character seemed really disappointed. Have you ever felt that way?"

This age group often processes experiences externally through narration, making them natural storytellers when given the right conditions.

Devon, father of seven- and nine-year-old siblings, notes: "Our breakthrough was creating a 'Dad and me' breakfast once a week with each kid. We go to the same diner, sit at the counter, and just hang out. Something about that special time, plus not facing each other directly at the counter, leads to these amazing conversations that never happen when I'm directly asking about their lives."

For Tweens and Teens (Ages 11–18)

Adolescents' communication needs include:

- respect for increased privacy while maintaining accessible connection

- text or other digital options for initiating sensitive conversations

- late-night openings when their circadian rhythms naturally favor disclosure

- conversation invitations without pressure for immediate or deep response

- driving time (Something about being in motion with minimal eye contact creates ideal conditions!)

This age group navigates a complex balance between connection needs and individuation. The conversation catcher respects this tension rather than fighting against it.

Zoe, mother of a 15-year-old, reflects: "I discovered that my son's most talkative time is around 10 p.m. when I'm exhausted. But when I started staying up just to be available during his natural 'opening up' window, our communication transformed. He knows I won't probe or lecture—I'm just there if he wants to talk. And increasingly, he does."

Common Conversation Blockers

Even with the best intentions, certain patterns reliably shut down communication. Here are the most common conversation killers and how to transform them:

The Advice Avalanche

This is when a child shares a problem and is immediately buried under solutions before they've fully expressed their experience. This communicates that you're more interested in fixing than understanding.

Transform it by: Using the "consultant" approach—asking if they want ideas before offering them: "That sounds challenging. Are you looking for suggestions, or did you just need someone to listen?" Honor their preference either way.

Maya, mother of an eight-year-old, shares: "My son would shut down whenever I jumped in with advice. Now, I ask, 'Do you want me to just listen, or would you like help solving this?' Nine times out of ten, he just wants me to listen. And ironically, after feeling heard, he's much more open to suggestions."

The Emotion Hijack

This is when your emotional reaction becomes bigger than the child's original sharing, making them regret opening up: "You did *what* at school today?!" or becoming visibly distressed by their struggle.

Transform it by: Managing your own emotional response first: "I appreciate you telling me that. I need a moment to think about it." Then process your reaction privately before responding to their disclosure.

William, father of a teenager, notes: "The hardest but most important thing I've learned is that my daughter doesn't need to carry my emotional reactions to her experiences. When she shares something concerning, I've trained myself to respond with curiosity rather than alarm. If I need to freak out, I do it later with my partner, not with her."

The Digging Operation

This is when one small disclosure triggers an excavation for more information: "Who else was there? What exactly did they say? Then what happened?" This interrogation style makes children feel investigated rather than understood.

Transform it by: Following their lead on disclosure depth. Match their energy and detail level rather than probing significantly deeper. If they share one detail, respond with interest but don't immediately demand five more.

Sonia, mother of a 10-year-old, reflects: "I realized I was treating casual mentions of school problems like a detective interviewing a witness. Now I try to match their disclosure level—if they mention something briefly, I acknowledge it briefly. If they elaborate, I follow their lead. They share so much more now that they don't fear triggering a full investigation."

The Lecture Launch

This is when a child's experience becomes a springboard for your speech about values, cautions, or life lessons. This transforms dialogue into a monologue and discourages future sharing.

Transform it by: Asking yourself, *Is there an actual question here?* If they haven't explicitly asked for guidance, focus on understanding rather than instructing. Save the teaching for a separate conversation if truly needed.

Marcus, father of three, shares: "I caught myself turning every mention of a friend's choice into a cautionary tale. My kids stopped telling me about their social lives entirely. Now I practice just saying, 'That's interesting' or asking a follow-up question instead of launching into 'Here's why that's concerning...' They've started sharing so much more."

Creating Conversation Rituals

While spontaneous openings for meaningful conversation are valuable, intentional rituals create reliable containers for connection. Consider implementing the following:

Daily Micro-Connection Points

Brief, reliable moments of potential sharing embedded in everyday routines:

- The 10-minute tuck-in chat with a specific prompt: "What made you feel proud today?"

- Car ride questions that become familiar but not rote: "What was different about today than you expected?"

- Meal sharing formats: rose (highlight), thorn (challenge), and bud (anticipation)

- Morning check-ins: "What's one thing you're looking forward to today?"

These micro-rituals signal ongoing interest without demanding deep disclosure every time.

Weekly Special Time

Dedicated one-on-one periods specifically designed for potential conversation:

- parent-child breakfast dates at a favorite café

- Sunday evening walks around the neighborhood

- Saturday morning pancake-making sessions

- monthly "adventure days" where you explore something new together

These special times build the relational foundation that makes deeper conversation possible.

Natural Transition Leveraging

Intentionally being present and available during key transitions that naturally lend themselves to sharing:

- The after-school decompression window: being fully available (not on devices) for the first 15 minutes after school

- The bedtime wind-down: building in buffer time for unexpected conversations

- The post-activity processing period: being present after sporting events, performances, or social gatherings

- The driving dividend: using car time for casual, low-pressure connection

These transition times often feature a neurobiological state shift that makes reflection and sharing more likely.

Liam, father of a nine-year-old, explains his approach: "I've learned that my daughter needs about 30 minutes of not talking about school after she gets home. If I respect that decompression time and just be nearby doing my own thing, she'll eventually start sharing these elaborate stories about her day. But if I pounce with questions the moment she walks in, I get nothing but grunts."

From Catching to Cultivating

The ultimate goal of the conversation catcher isn't just to hear about your child's day. It's to build a lifelong foundation of open communication that will serve them through all of life's complexities.

When children experience the safety of being truly heard without judgment, interruption, or hijacking, they develop both the capacity and the desire for authentic communication. This skill transfers far beyond your relationship with them—it shapes how they communicate in friendships, romantic relationships, educational settings, and eventually their own parenting.

You're not just catching conversations today; you're cultivating communication capabilities that will last a lifetime.

Erin, mother of now-adult children, reflects: "The investment in creating those conversation rituals when my kids were young has paid dividends I never imagined. Now in their twenties, they still call regularly to process challenges and celebrate victories. They've told me that knowing how to talk about hard things has been one of their greatest advantages in adult relationships. It all started with those bedtime chats and dinner table questions."

In the next chapter, we'll explore the emotional coach—how to guide children through their feelings without being overwhelmed by them, building emotional intelligence that will serve them throughout life.

Quick tip: Side-by-side activities often yield deeper conversations than face-to-face questions. Try walking, driving, or working on a project together, then listen with curiosity rather than jumping in with advice or solutions.

Conversation Catcher Reflection Questions

1. When and where does your child currently seem most open to conversation?

2. Which conversation blockers do you most often find yourself using?

3. What's one conversation ritual you could implement this week?

4. How might your own childhood experiences with being heard (or not) influence your conversation patterns with your children?

5. What conversation topics feel most difficult for you to navigate calmly?

Tool 6:
The Emotional Coach

Your four-year-old is writhing on the floor of the grocery store, screaming about the candy you wouldn't buy. Your nine-year-old slams their bedroom door after receiving a disappointing grade. Your teenager storms out of the house when you set a boundary about weekend plans.

In these moments of emotional intensity, what's your default response?

Many of us were raised with approaches like this:

- "Stop crying or I'll give you something to cry about."

- "You're overreacting. It's not that bad."

- "Just calm down and be reasonable!"

- "Go to your room until you can control yourself."

These responses share a common thread—they dismiss, minimize, or punish emotions rather than teaching children how to understand and manage them. They reflect an outdated belief that emotions are inconvenient disruptions to be suppressed rather than valuable data to be processed.

The emotional coach tool offers a radically different approach. Instead of seeing emotions as problems to eliminate, emotional coaching treats feelings as opportunities for connection and learning. This doesn't mean permitting all behaviors or abandoning boundaries. Instead, it means acknowledging emotions as valuable information that helps children understand themselves while teaching them how to express those feelings in healthy ways.

The Five Elements of Emotional Coaching

The emotional coach approach consists of five key elements that work together to build emotional intelligence in children of all ages. This framework is based on decades of research in emotional development and practical application across diverse families.

The Awareness Foundation

Emotional coaching begins with your own emotional awareness. This means:

- recognizing your own emotional reactions to your child's feelings

- understanding your emotional history and triggers

- developing comfort with the full range of emotions, including difficult ones

- building your capacity to stay present during emotional intensity

This foundation is essential because we can only coach what we can recognize and tolerate. Many parents find certain emotions particularly challenging based on their own upbringing and experiences.

Claire, mother of an emotional six-year-old, shares: "I realized I responded terribly to my son's anger because anger was forbidden in my childhood home. When I acknowledged this pattern, I could start building my own capacity to stay present when he was angry rather than shutting him down like my parents did to me."

The Emotional Connection

Before any teaching or guidance can occur, children need to feel their emotions are valid and understood. This connection includes:

- recognizing emotional moments as opportunities for closeness rather than problems

- giving full attention to the child during emotional episodes

- showing empathy through body language, tone, and presence

- avoiding dismissal or minimization of any feeling

This connection serves as emotional first aid, creating the safety needed for learning and growth.

Marcus, father of a sensitive four-year-old, reflects: "I used to immediately try to fix my daughter's upsets or distract her from them. I've learned that simply sitting with her, maintaining gentle eye contact, and saying 'I see you're really sad' helps her feel understood in a way that my solutions never did."

The Validation Bridge

Children need explicit confirmation that their emotions make sense and are acceptable. This validation includes:

- Naming the observed emotion: "It looks like you're feeling disappointed."

- Normalizing the feeling: "It makes sense you'd feel that way."

- Separating feelings from behaviors: "It's completely okay to feel angry. It's not okay to hit."

- Avoiding judgment about the emotion itself: Never "You shouldn't feel jealous," but rather "Jealousy can feel really uncomfortable, can't it?"

This validation builds emotional literacy—the ability to identify and articulate feelings, which research shows is the foundation for emotional regulation.

Sophia, mother of two, notes: "The phrase 'It makes sense you feel that way' has transformed our household. My boys went from hiding their difficult feelings to talking about them openly because they no longer fear being told they're wrong for feeling what they feel."

The Empowerment Process

Once emotions are recognized and validated, children can learn to work with them effectively. This empowerment includes:

- teaching emotional vocabulary beyond the basics of mad, sad, and glad

- exploring body sensations connected to different feelings

- developing personalized calming strategies that work for each child's temperament

- practicing emotional skills during calm times, not just during upsets

- building confidence in the child's growing ability to understand and manage feelings

This process transforms emotions from overwhelming experiences to manageable states with useful information.

Jamal, father of a nine-year-old with anxiety, shares: "We created a 'calm down toolkit' with my son—specific breathing exercises, a stress ball, and visualization techniques. We practice when he's already calm, which makes the tools more accessible during actual anxious moments. He's gone from being overwhelmed by worry to saying 'My body's telling me I'm worried. I know what to do.'"

The Problem-Solving Partnership

The final element addresses the situation that triggered the emotion, but only after the emotional processing has occurred. This partnership includes:

- helping the child identify their goals in the situation

- brainstorming possible solutions together

- evaluating different options while respecting the child's growing autonomy

- supporting implementation of their chosen approach

- reflecting together on what worked and what didn't

This collaborative problem-solving teaches children that emotions provide important information about needs and values, which can then guide effective action.

Eve, mother of a 12-year-old, explains: "When my son was devastated about not making the basketball team, we moved through the entire process—acknowledging the disappointment, validating how much it hurt, using calming strategies, and then, days later when he was ready, exploring his options. He ultimately decided to join a community league and get additional coaching. The key was not rushing to problem-solving before the emotion itself had been processed."

Emotional Coaching Across Development

While the core framework remains consistent, implementation shifts across different developmental stages:

For Toddlers and Preschoolers (Ages 2–5)

Young children need emotional coaching that:

- uses simple emotional vocabulary: happy, sad, mad, scared, excited

- connects feelings to observable body states: "Your hands are in fists. You look mad."

- offers concrete physical comfort alongside validation

- provides very simple calming strategies: deep breaths, sensory tools, physical movement

- maintains clear behavior boundaries while accepting all feelings

At this age, children's emotional reactions are often intense and physical because their brains have not yet developed the capacity for more sophisticated regulation. Your calm presence serves as their external regulation system.

Tara, mother of a three-year-old, shares: "I think of myself as my daughter's emotional training wheels. She physically needs my calm body and voice to help her regain balance during big feelings. Simple techniques like 'smell the flower, blow out the candle' for deep breathing help her build those beginning self-regulation skills."

For School-Age Children (Ages 6–10)

Elementary-aged children benefit from coaching that:

- expands emotional vocabulary significantly: disappointed, frustrated, anxious, proud

- makes connections between thoughts, feelings, and behaviors explicit

- teaches multiple calming strategies to try in different contexts

- involves more collaborative problem-solving after emotions are processed

- helps identify emotional patterns: "I've noticed you often feel nervous before tests."

This age group develops increased metacognition—the ability to think about their own thinking and feeling processes—making this an ideal time to build emotional awareness.

Richard, father of an eight-year-old, notes: "My son used to get overwhelmed by frustration during homework. We created a visual feelings thermometer where he could identify when his frustration was getting too hot. Having that visual reference helped him catch his emotions earlier and use his calming strategies before complete meltdown."

For Tweens and Teens (Ages 11–18)

Adolescents need emotional coaching that:

- respects increased privacy needs while maintaining connection

- acknowledges complex and sometimes contradictory emotions

- balances validation with growing independence

- supports development of personally meaningful coping strategies

- recognizes the impact of physiological changes on emotional experiences

The adolescent brain undergoes significant development, particularly in areas related to emotional processing. Teens may swing between childlike emotional needs and adult-like independence, sometimes within minutes.

Daria, mother of a 14-year-old, reflects: "I've learned to read my daughter's cues for when she wants to process emotions together versus when she needs space. I might simply say, 'Looks like a rough day. I'm here if you want to talk,' and then respect her choice either way. When she does open up, I focus completely on understanding rather than directing or fixing."

Common Emotional Coaching Challenges

Even with the best intentions, emotional coaching faces obstacles. Here's how to navigate common challenges when applying these research-backed techniques:

When Emotions Feel Too Big

Some emotional expressions—screaming tantrums, aggressive outbursts, complete withdrawal—can feel overwhelming to coach. When emotions seem too intense, do this:

- Remember that the biggest emotions need coaching the most.

- Focus first on your own regulation. You can't coach what you can't tolerate.

- Use fewer words and more calming presence as intensity increases.

- Ensure physical safety first, emotional processing second.

- Accept that big feelings take time to process—resolution isn't always immediate.

The goal isn't to quickly end the emotional expression but to support the child through the full arc of the feeling.

Michael, father of a highly sensitive child, shares: "My breakthrough came when I stopped seeing my son's meltdowns as something to shut down and started seeing them as storms we needed to weather together. I'd say, 'This is a big feeling. I'm right here with you until it passes.' Sometimes it takes 30 minutes, but he always comes through more regulated and connected when I stay steady through the process."

When Emotions Trigger Your Own History

Our responses to children's emotions are profoundly shaped by how our emotions were handled in childhood. When you find yourself strongly triggered:

- Acknowledge your reaction internally: "This is bringing up my own stuff."

- Create brief space to regulate if necessary: "I need a moment to think."

- Return to presence with renewed perspective.

- Consider your own emotional healing needs separate from the parenting moment.

- Use triggering interactions as information about where you might need support.

Your ability to coach emotions you struggle with personally can grow with awareness and practice.

Aiden, father of three, reflects: "I used to completely shut down when my kids expressed sadness—I'd immediately try to cheer them up or minimize it. Through therapy, I realized my parents always dismissed my sadness as weakness, so I never learned how to tolerate it. Now I can sit with my children's sadness without needing to fix it immediately, though it's still the hardest emotion for me."

When Cultural Contexts Create Complexity

Families navigate diverse cultural expectations around emotional expression. When dominant emotional coaching models feel culturally misaligned, try this:

- Honor the emotional wisdom within your cultural tradition.

- Consider which elements of emotional coaching complement your values.

- Adapt language and approaches to fit your family's cultural context.

- Recognize the universal human need for emotional understanding.

- Balance cultural continuity with evolving understanding of emotional development.

Emotional coaching isn't one-size-fits-all; it should respect and incorporate diverse cultural approaches to emotional well-being.

Lin, mother of two, explains: "In my Chinese-American family, we value emotional restraint in certain contexts while still wanting our children to develop emotional intelligence. I've adapted emotional coaching to honor both traditions—we have private spaces for processing big feelings rather than public ones, and we emphasize how emotional awareness serves collective harmony as well as individual well-being."

Building Your Emotional Coaching Practice

Start implementing the emotional coach with these practical steps:

Create an Emotions-Welcome Home

Establish an environment where all feelings are acceptable, even when certain behaviors aren't:

- Use emotion-positive language: "It's okay to feel angry," while maintaining behavior boundaries: "It's not okay to hit."

- Post visual reminders about emotions: feelings charts, calming strategy menus, facial expression guides.

- Normalize emotional expression through books, discussions, and your own appropriate sharing.

- Develop family language for emotional states: "I'm in the red zone" or "My engine is running too high."

This emotions-welcome atmosphere provides the foundation for all specific coaching strategies.

Build Your Personal Emotion Regulation Toolkit

You can't coach what you can't manage in yourself:

- Identify your emotional triggers and early warning signs.

- Develop personal regulation strategies that work for your nervous system.

- Create micro-breaks for regulation during intense parenting moments.

- Build support systems for processing your own emotional needs.

- Practice self-compassion when you struggle with emotional regulation.

Your growing regulation capabilities directly enhance your emotional coaching effectiveness.

Practice the Coaching Sequence

The basic sequence remains consistent across situations:

- Notice and approach emotional moments: "I see you're having some big feelings."

- Validate the emotion: "It makes sense you feel disappointed."

- Offer support for regulation: "Would deep breaths help, or would you like some space?"

- Problem-solve when appropriate: "When you're ready, we can figure out what to do next."

Start with low-intensity emotions to build your confidence before tackling more challenging situations.

Create Calming Spaces and Tools

Physical supports enhance emotional coaching:

- Designate a calming corner with comfortable seating, sensory tools, and visual supports.

- Develop personalized calming kits for each child based on their preferences.

- Make calming tools accessible throughout your home.

- Introduce tools during calm times, practicing together before they're needed in crisis.

- Regularly update tools as children develop and their needs change.

These concrete resources make emotional regulation skills tangible for children still developing abstract thinking.

Schedule Emotional Check-Ins

Proactive connection strengthens emotional coaching:

- Create regular one-on-one time for emotional temperature checks.

- Use visual tools like mood meters or feeling thermometers for daily reflection.

- Develop family rituals for sharing feelings: rose/thorn/bud at dinner, bedtime reflections.

- Notice and celebrate growing emotional skills: "I saw how you calmed yourself down today."

- Model appropriate emotional sharing: "I felt frustrated when I was stuck in traffic today."

These proactive practices build emotional awareness during calm periods, making intense moments easier to navigate.

The emotional coach isn't about creating perfect emotional regulation in your children (or yourself). It's about developing an environment where emotions are valued as information, processed with compassion, and gradually integrated into a balanced life. Even imperfect emotional coaching—coaching punctuated by your own emotional moments and learning edges—is transformative when offered with authenticity and repair.

Lisa, a mother of now-adult children, reflects: "Looking back on two decades of parenting, I believe emotional coaching was the most important gift I gave my children. They've told me that knowing how to recognize, name, and manage their feelings has helped them navigate everything from relationships to career challenges. I wasn't perfect at it—I had plenty of moments where I lost my cool or missed emotional cues—but the consistent message that feelings matter and can be managed has served them throughout their lives."

In the next chapter, we'll explore the routine reset—how to create daily structures that prevent chaos and support everyone's well-being.

Quick tip: Validate feelings before problem-solving: "It makes sense you feel disappointed." This validates emotions without condoning behaviors, helping children develop emotional literacy—the foundation for self-regulation.

Emotional Coach Reflection Questions

1. Which emotions are most challenging for you to respond to calmly in your children?

2. How were your emotions handled in your family of origin?

3. What calming strategies work best for you personally?

4. Which element of emotional coaching feels most natural to you, and which feels most challenging?

5. How might increased emotional coaching impact your family culture?

TOOL 7:
THE ROUTINE RESET

The morning madness has become your daily nightmare. Six requests for breakfast amid forgotten homework, misplaced shoes, and inexplicable dawdling. By the time everyone exits the house, you've yelled three times, threatened twice, and fantasized about running away to a deserted island where no one asks you to find their other sock.

Or perhaps it's the bedtime battlefield that's breaking you. What should be a gentle wind-down becomes a two-hour marathon of negotiations, stalling tactics, and meltdowns—yours and theirs.

If these scenarios sound painfully familiar, you're experiencing what I call "structural stress," the tension that arises not from differences in parenting philosophy or discipline challenges, but from the fundamental organization of your family's day.

The routine reset tool addresses this often-overlooked source of parent-child conflict by creating intentional structures that support everyone's needs. It's not about rigid schedules or Pinterest-perfect systems. It's about designing daily rhythms that work with human nature rather than against it, reducing friction points and creating space for connection.

The Neuroscience of Routines

The human brain, regardless of age, craves predictability. Neuroscience research shows that when we can anticipate what's coming next, our nervous systems remain in a state of regulated calm rather than hypervigilant stress[12]. For children, whose prefrontal cortex (the brain's planning center) is still developing, this predictability is even more crucial.

When children can predict the flow of their day, several remarkable brain benefits occur:

- The amygdala (fear center) shows decreased activation.

- Stress hormones like cortisol maintain healthier baseline levels.

- Cognitive resources are freed for learning rather than consumed by anxiety.

- The brain builds stronger executive function through repeated sequences.

- Emotional regulation capacity increases with environmental predictability.

Dr. Bruce Perry, renowned child psychiatrist, explains: "Predictable, patterned experiences build the neural networks that help a child regulate emotional states and support healthy development. The brain is a pattern-seeking organ, and

---

[12] Grupe & Nitschke, 2013

routines provide the patterns it needs to organize information efficiently[13]."

This neurobiological reality explains why even children who resist routines often thrive once they're established. Their resistance isn't to structure itself, but to the stress of transitions or the fear of losing autonomy within that structure.

The Four Elements of Effective Routines

The routine reset approach consists of four key elements that create structures children can both rely on and grow within:

The Rhythm Foundation

Effective family routines are built on recognizing natural rhythms rather than imposing arbitrary schedules. This means:

- honoring biological timing: energy peaks and valleys, natural wake/sleep windows

- structuring days around predictable patterns rather than rigid clock times

- creating consistent sequence anchors even when timing shifts

- allowing appropriate flexibility within a reliable framework

- aligning routines with developmental capabilities, not external expectations

---

[13] Cooke Douglas, 2021

This rhythm foundation respects human nature while providing the structure children need.

Amir, father of three, shares: "I was trying to enforce a rigid 7:30 p.m. bedtime for all my kids, which created constant battles. When I shifted to a consistent bedtime sequence that started earlier for my youngest and later for my pre-teen, while keeping the steps the same, bedtime battles decreased dramatically. The predictable rhythm, not the exact timing, was what mattered most."

The Visual-Verbal-Physical System

Children process routine expectations most effectively when information comes through multiple channels:

- Visual supports: charts, photographs, drawings of routine steps

- Verbal cues: consistent language signals like "Five-minute warning" or "Next comes..."

- Physical environment design: items organized in sequence, spaces designated for specific activities

- Multisensory transitions: songs, movements, or sensory experiences that signal shifts

This multi-channel system reduces the need for constant adult direction and builds children's independence within structure.

Lydia, mother of a five-year-old, explains: "My breakthrough came when I created a morning routine chart with photos of each step. Suddenly, my son could manage his own sequence without me nagging. I still give gentle reminders, but he can look at the visual guide and know exactly what comes next. It's like he finally has a map for his day."

The Connection Points

Strategic moments of connection embedded within routines transform them from mechanical processes to relationship-building opportunities:

- Morning magic: brief but fully present greeting routines to start the day

- Special signals at transition moments: secret handshakes, special phrases

- Micro-connection rituals before separations: the three-kiss goodbye, the squeezy hug

- End-of-day reconnection rituals: the highlight/lowlight share, the gratitude moment

- Sensory soothing: physical touch anchors appropriate to your child's preferences

These connection points take seconds but dramatically increase cooperation by meeting the attachment needs that often underlie resistance.

Carlos, father of two, notes: "I discovered that a 30-second 'Daddy snuggle' at the start of bedtime routine completely transformed my daughters' cooperation with the rest of the steps. That brief moment of connection seems to fill their attachment tanks enough to move through teeth-brushing and pajamas without the usual resistance."

The Autonomy Balance

Effective routines balance predictable structure with appropriate choice and control for children:

- offering structured choices within routines. ("Bath before or after story?")

- creating visual choice menus for certain routine elements

- involving children in routine design. ("What helps you feel ready for bedtime?")

- designating certain routine elements as child-directed

- adjusting control levels based on developmental readiness

This autonomy balance prevents power struggles by meeting children's developmental need for agency while maintaining necessary structure.

Sophia, mother of a strong-willed four-year-old, shares: "My son fought bedtime relentlessly until I created a 'bedtime choice board' where he could select the order of certain steps, choose between two pajama options, and pick the books. The bedtime sequence still happens reliably, but now he feels ownership of the process instead of being controlled by it."

Designing Routines for Developmental Stages

Effective routines evolve with your child's changing capabilities and needs:

For Toddlers and Preschoolers (Ages 2–5)

Young children thrive with routines that:

- Use concrete visual supports: photographs of the child completing each step

- Keep sequences brief: 3-5 steps maximum before a natural break

- Incorporate playfulness: songs, puppets, or games within routine steps

- Use more than one cue: feature physical guidance alongside verbal cues

- Unfold the same way: maintain extreme consistency in sequence, if not exact timing

At this stage, children have limited abstract thinking and time perception. Their cooperation depends on predictable patterns more than reasoning.

Maya, mother of a three-year-old, notes: "I created a morning routine chart with actual photos of my daughter doing each step—brushing teeth, getting dressed, eating breakfast. The visual reminders transformed our mornings from constant nagging to her proudly following her 'big girl steps.' She can't tell time yet, but she understands sequence perfectly."

For School-Age Children (Ages 6–10)

Elementary-aged children benefit from routines that:

- Balance structure with increasing autonomy: checklists they manage themselves

- Include their input in routine design: "What would help our mornings work better?"

- Feature growing responsibility for time management: personal alarm clocks, timers

- Include both individual and family components: personal morning preparations followed by family breakfast

- Connect routines to meaningful outcomes: "When we follow our homework routine, we have more time for games afterward."

This age group thrives when routines help them develop competence and responsibility within a reliable structure.

Jackson, father of an eight-year-old, shares: "The game-changer was creating a laminated after-school checklist my son manages himself. It includes snack, homework, instrument practice, and chores—he can choose the order but knows all elements need to happen before screen time. My nagging has decreased by about 90%, and he's developing actual time management skills."

For Tweens and Teens (Ages 11–18)

Adolescents need routines that:

- respect their increasing need for autonomy while maintaining structure

- focus on outcomes rather than micromanaging processes. ("Assignment completion" versus "Sit at desk for one hour")

- include their active participation in creating and adjusting systems

- balance growing independence with family connection points

- allow for natural consequences of routine lapses with supportive guidance

This age group navigates a complex balance between developing adult-like independence and still needing supportive structures.

Elena, mother of a 15-year-old, reflects: "My son and I co-created his study routine based on when his brain works best—which turns out to be later than I'd prefer! Instead of fighting his natural rhythm, we structured family dinner at a consistent time, then he has his independent study block afterward. The key was involving him in the design rather than imposing my preferred schedule."

Strategic Routines for Challenging Transitions

Certain daily transitions consistently generate more stress than others. Here's how to transform the most common friction points:

The Morning Launch

Mornings often combine time pressure with sleep inertia to create perfect storm conditions. Effective morning routines:

- Begin the night before: backpacks packed, clothes selected, lunch components prepped

- Create buffer zones rather than exact minute schedules: "Before breakfast" versus "7:15 a.m."

- Minimize decision-making: consistent breakfast options, designated clothing spaces

- Build in independent activities for early risers: special quiet-time boxes or designated morning activities

- Include connection before direction: brief snuggle time before the sequence begins

The key is creating a system that requires minimal parental supervision while meeting everyone's basic needs efficiently.

Tara, mother of three, explains: "My breakthrough came when I realized I was the bottleneck in our morning routine—everyone needed me simultaneously. Now, each child has their own visual morning checklist, while I focus on being a calm presence rather than the director of the show. We also moved the most challenging steps to the night before, which made mornings significantly smoother."

The After-School Transition

The period immediately after school combines fatigue, hunger, and emotional processing needs, creating vulnerability to meltdowns. Effective after-school routines:

- Start with physiological regulation: snack, movement, sensory needs.

- Build in decompression time: before questions or homework.

- Create consistent belonging rituals: special greetings, brief connection moments.

- Balance structure with downtime: appropriate to each child's needs.

- Separate social processing from task demands: connection before direction.

This transition benefits from recognizing the significant energy children expend during school hours and their need to reset before further demands.

Miguel, father of two, shares: "I noticed my girls were melting down right after school. Our new routine is simple: protein snack in the car, 20 minutes of outdoor physical play at home, then a 10-minute quiet period with books or drawing before any homework begins. This sequence addresses their physical needs first, then gives them space to decompress. Homework battles have virtually disappeared."

The Dinner and Evening Sequence

The end-of-day period often combines everyone's accumulated fatigue with complex logistical demands. Effective evening routines:

- Establish prep rituals that involve children appropriately: setting table, simple food prep.

- Create clear beginning and ending signals: handwashing ritual, gratitude practice.

- Separate eating from behavior management: focusing on connection during meals.

- Mind the in-between: building in reasonable transition time between activities.

- Calm down slowly: designing wind-down sequences that gradually reduce stimulation.

Evening routines that thoughtfully address sensory, nutritional, and connection needs prevent the escalation cycle that often leads to bedtime battles.

Amara, mother of a six-year-old, notes: "We created a post-dinner 'power hour' with a visual timer—30 minutes of active family play followed by 30 minutes of calm activities like puzzles or reading. This structured transition between dinner energy and bedtime calm has completely transformed our evenings from chaos to connection."

The Bedtime Journey

Perhaps the most challenging transition is the shift from wakefulness to sleep, which requires both physiological and psychological changes. Effective bedtime routines:

- follow consistent sequence regardless of exact timing

- gradually reduce stimulation: active play → quiet play → passive activities

- address physical needs methodically: hunger, thirst, bathroom, temperature

- include both practical tasks and connection activities

- end with brief, reliable attachment rituals: special phrases, predictable affection

Effective bedtime routines recognize that sleep is not a switch to be flipped but a journey to be supported through consistent cues.

David, father of a sleep-resistant four-year-old, reflects: "We were locked in epic bedtime battles until we created our 'sleepy train' routine—a consistent six-step sequence where each activity is a 'station' on the journey to sleep. The physical metaphor of a train moving between stations helps him visualize the process, and the predictability has virtually eliminated the resistance. He still occasionally negotiates for 'one more book,' but the overall structure creates security that actually helps him relax into sleep."

Troubleshooting Your Routine Reset

Even well-designed routines encounter challenges. Here's how to navigate common obstacles:

When Routines Meet Resistance

Initial pushback against new structures is normal and doesn't indicate failure. When children resist routines:

- Distinguish between transition discomfort and actual system problems.

- Maintain calm consistency through the initial adjustment period (typically 2–3 weeks).

- Look for small successes rather than perfect implementation.

- Address legitimate concerns with adjustments rather than abandonment.

- Remember that resistance often peaks just before acceptance.

Children test new systems to verify reliability before investing in the changed pattern.

Keisha, mother of three, shares: "When we implemented our new morning routine, the resistance was intense for about ten days. I almost gave up, thinking it wasn't working. Then suddenly, on day 11, everyone started following the system with minimal reminders. They needed to test whether I would remain consistent before adapting to the new pattern."

When Special Circumstances Disrupt Routines

Life inevitably includes disruptions through illness, travel, special events, or unexpected situations. When routines face temporary disruption:

- Acknowledge the change explicitly: "Today will be different because..."

- Maintain key anchors even when full routines aren't possible: consistency in connection rituals, simplified versions of essential sequences.

- Create special circumstance mini-routines: travel routines, sick day modifications.

- Return to regular routines: promptly with clear transition language.

- Process significant disruptions: both beforehand and afterward.

Flexibility within a reliable overall structure helps children navigate necessary changes without losing the security of predictability.

James, father of a routine-dependent child, explains: "Our son struggles with changes, so we created what we call 'adventure day rules' versus 'regular day rules.' Before trips or special events, we review which parts of our routine will stay the same and which will change. Having language for these differences has helped him adapt to necessary variations without feeling completely unmoored."

When Adults Have Different Routine Preferences

Co-parents or caregivers may have different approaches to structure and routine. When adults disagree:

- Focus on outcomes rather than specific implementations: "Children ready on time" versus "Follow exact seven-step process."

- Identify core non-negotiable elements while allowing flexibility in style.

- Create visual supports that work across caregiver contexts.

- Avoid undermining other adults' approaches in front of children.

- Recognize that some routine variations can build adaptability.

The goal is consistency in essential elements while allowing for different but equally valid approaches to implementation.

Lin, co-parenting after divorce, reflects: "Initially, I was frustrated that my ex-husband's morning routine differed from mine. Then I realized our approaches both worked, just differently. We agreed on the essential outcomes—teeth brushed, appropriate clothes, breakfast eaten, on time for school—while accepting that the process could vary between homes. The kids have actually developed flexibility from navigating both systems."

Building Your Family's Routine System

Start implementing the routine reset with these practical steps:

Conduct a Friction Audit

Before designing new routines, assess your current reality:

- Track for one week: When do power struggles consistently occur?

- Identify physiological factors: Was there hunger, fatigue, sensory overload moments?

- Notice transition challenges: Which shifts consistently create tension?

- Consider temperament factors: Where do your children's natural tendencies clash with current expectations?

- Reflect on parent pain points: Which daily moments consistently frustrate you?

This assessment provides the foundation for targeted improvements rather than arbitrary changes.

Choose One Routine Reset Focus

Rather than overhauling everything simultaneously, select the most problematic transition:

- Identify the highest-stress daily transition.

- Commit to maintaining other routines while focusing on improvement efforts.

- Set realistic expectations for adjustment periods.

- Gather necessary supplies before implementation.

- Prepare language to introduce the changes in a positive way.

This focused approach prevents overwhelm while creating momentum through visible success.

Design Your Routine Blueprint

Create a clear structure for your chosen routine:

- List all necessary components in logical sequence.

- Break complex routines into distinct phases with clear transitions.

- Identify appropriate autonomy opportunities.

- Plan connection points within the structure.

- Create necessary visual or environmental supports.

This blueprint translates good intentions into implementable systems.

Implement With Preparation and Persistence

Introduce your routine reset thoughtfully:

- Explain the new routine during a calm moment, not during the transition itself.

- Use positive framing: "Our new system will help everyone feel less rushed."

- Demonstrate components that might be unfamiliar.

- Express confidence in the process and your child's capabilities.

- Maintain matter-of-fact consistency through initial resistance.

This implementation approach sets the tone for successful adaptation.

Refine Based on Real-World Results

After 1–2 weeks of implementation:

- Assess what's working and what needs adjustment.

- Make targeted modifications rather than complete overhauls.

- Involve children in problem-solving persistent challenges.

- Celebrate improvements, even if the routine isn't yet perfect.

- Continue evolving the system as developmental needs change.

This iterative approach allows your routines to grow with your family rather than becoming rigid obstacles.

The routine reset isn't about creating a perfectly orchestrated household where children move robotically through their days. It's about designing intentional structures that reduce unnecessary friction, support developmental needs, and create space for connection rather than conflict. When daily transitions flow more smoothly, both children and parents have more emotional energy for the relationships that matter most.

Sara, mother of three ranging from three to twelve, reflects after six months of routine implementation: "The most surprising outcome wasn't just the practical improvements—though those were significant. The real transformation was emotional. When we're not constantly battling through transitions, we actually enjoy each other more. Our home feels less like a battleground and more like a sanctuary where we all know what to expect and can relax into connection."

In the next chapter, we'll explore the repair ritual—how to rebuild trust and strengthen relationships after inevitable ruptures occur.

Quick tip: Predictable routines reduce power struggles by working with, not against, the brain's need for pattern and predictability. Create visual schedules children can follow, reducing the need for constant parental direction.

Routine Reset Reflection Questions

1. Which daily transition consistently creates the most stress in your family?

2. How might your child's temperament and developmental stage affect their routine needs?

3. What elements of routine do you personally find supportive versus constraining?

4. What's one small routine adjustment you could implement this week?

5. How might more effective routines change the emotional atmosphere in your home?

Tool 8:
The Repair Ritual

It happened again.

Despite your best intentions, despite all the tools we've explored in previous chapters, you lost your cool. Maybe you yelled at your child for spilling juice on the carpet. Perhaps you said something in frustration that you immediately wished you could take back. Or possibly you enforced a boundary with harsh energy that left everyone feeling awful.

Now what?

If you're like most parents, your immediate internal reaction is likely a combination of guilt, shame, and self-criticism. *I'm a terrible parent. I've traumatized my child. I'll never get this right.*

But what if these inevitable ruptures in your relationship weren't the disasters they feel like in the moment? What if they were opportunities for some of the most powerful connections and learning possible?

That's exactly what the repair ritual provides—a framework for transforming parenting mistakes into relationship-strengthening moments that build resilience, trust, and emotional intelligence.

The Science of Rupture and Repair

For decades, attachment researchers have studied what creates secure relationships between parents and children. What they've discovered challenges our perfectionist parenting culture: It's not perfect attunement that creates secure attachment, but rather the consistent repair of inevitable misattunements[14].

Dr. Ed Tronick's famous still face experiment demonstrates this beautifully. When mothers briefly stopped responding to their babies and presented a still, expressionless face, the babies became distressed. But when mothers resumed normal, responsive interaction, the relationship rapidly repaired. This natural rupture-and-repair sequence happens hundreds of times in healthy parent-child relationships[15].

In fact, neuroscience research shows that these repair cycles create particularly strong neural connections in children's developing brains. When a child experiences distress followed by reconnection, their nervous system receives powerful training in resilience—the ability to return to balance after disruption[16].

Dr. Dan Siegel, clinical professor of psychiatry, explains: "Repair doesn't just heal the immediate disconnect—it actually strengthens the relationship beyond its pre-rupture state,

---

[14] Feldman, 2017
[15] Tronick et al., 1978; Streep, 2023
[16] Schwartz, n.d.

creating what I call a 'secure attachment scar' that enhances resilience over time"[17].

This research offers tremendous liberation from parenting perfectionism. The goal isn't to never rupture—that's both impossible and undesirable for your child's development. The goal is to repair consistently and effectively when ruptures inevitably occur.

The Four Elements of Effective Repair

The repair ritual consists of four key elements that transform relationship ruptures into opportunities for connection and growth. This approach works with children of all ages and across diverse cultural contexts.

The Cooling Pause

Effective repair begins with a brief pause that allows both you and your child to regain some physiological and emotional regulation:

- Create brief physical distance if needed: "I need a moment to calm down."

- Use simple self-regulation techniques: deep breathing, physical grounding.

- Allow initial emotional intensity to decrease for both parties.

---

[17] Siegel, n.d.

- Signal that conversation will continue: "We'll talk about this when we're both feeling calmer."

- Resist the urge to immediately fix the situation while still emotionally flooded.

This pause isn't abandonment or stonewalling—it's responsible recognition that repair conversations require some basic regulation to be effective.

Amir, father of three, shares: "I used to try to force immediate repair when I'd yelled, which often made things worse because neither of us was regulated. Now I say, 'I'm feeling too frustrated to talk well right now. I'm going to take five minutes to calm down, and then we'll figure this out together.' That brief pause makes all the difference in how the repair unfolds."

The Authentic Acknowledgment

Once basic regulation is established, effective repair requires honest acknowledgment of what occurred:

- Take clear responsibility for your part: "I yelled when I was frustrated."

- Use specific, behavioral language rather than vague apologies.

- Avoid justifications that undermine the acknowledgment: "I'm sorry I yelled, BUT you weren't listening."

- Separate intent from impact: "I didn't mean to scare you, and I see that I did."

- Model appropriate vulnerability without emotional flooding.

This acknowledgment demonstrates emotional responsibility and integrity rather than perfectionism or defensiveness.

Sarah, mother of a sensitive seven-year-old, reflects: "I realized my 'apologies' were actually justifications—'I'm sorry I yelled, but you pushed my buttons.' When I shifted to simply acknowledging my behavior without qualifiers—'I raised my voice and used words that weren't respectful'—my daughter's whole demeanor changed. She could feel the authenticity."

The Reconnection Bridge

After acknowledgment comes the active rebuilding of emotional connection:

- Offer physical reconnection if welcomed: hug, hand on shoulder, sitting close.

- Express the core relationship message: "I love you no matter what."

- Separate behavior from worth: "I didn't like the behavior, but I always love you."

- Recognize mutual participation when appropriate: "We both had big feelings."

- Create space for the child's experience: "How did that feel for you?"

This reconnection step addresses the attachment anxiety that ruptures often trigger, reassuring children that the relationship remains secure despite imperfect interactions.

Miguel, father of a four-year-old, shares: "My breakthrough came when I realized my son needed explicit reassurance after I'd lost my temper. Now I make sure to say, 'I love you even when I'm angry. Nothing changes that.' I can literally see his body relax when he hears those words."

The Forward Integration

The final element focuses on learning and growth rather than dwelling in guilt or shame:

- Explore better future approaches: "Next time we could..."

- Identify triggers or patterns when helpful: "I notice I get frustrated when we're running late."

- Connect to values: "In our family, we treat each other with respect, even in hard moments."

- Express confidence in ongoing growth: "We're both learning."

- Close the repair loop definitively rather than letting it linger.

This integration transforms the rupture from a parenting failure into a growth opportunity for everyone involved.

Emma, mother of three, notes: "The game-changer was when I stopped seeing repairs as evidence of my inadequacy and started seeing them as powerful teaching moments. Now, after acknowledging a mistake, I might say, 'What could we both do differently next time?' My kids often have surprisingly insightful suggestions, and they're learning that relationships can heal after conflicts."

Repair Across Developmental Stages

While the core elements remain consistent, implementation shifts across developmental stages:

For Toddlers and Preschoolers (Ages 2–5)

Young children need repair that:

- uses simple, concrete language ("I used a loud voice. That was scary.")

- includes physical reconnection when welcome: hugs, gentle touch

- happens relatively soon after the rupture due to limited time perception

- doesn't require verbal processing from the child unless offered

- focuses on emotional safety restoration rather than explanation

At this age, children need to experience repair more than understand the concept of it. Your calm presence and reconnection behaviors speak louder than words.

Lydia, mother of a three-year-old, explains: "After I snapped at my daughter, I knelt down to her eye level, spoke in a gentle voice, and simply said, 'Mommy used a scary voice. I'm sorry. I love you.' Then I opened my arms for a hug if she wanted one. The simplicity and physical connection helped her feel safe again without overwhelming her with explanations her brain isn't ready to process."

For School-Age Children (Ages 6–10)

Elementary-aged children benefit from repair that:

- Acknowledges specific impacts: "I interrupted you when you were trying to tell me something important."

- Invites their experience: "How did you feel when that happened?"

- Involves collaborative problem-solving: "What might work better next time?"

- Includes clear closure: "Do you feel better about what happened now?"

- Balances responsibility appropriately: "I shouldn't have yelled, AND we still need to work on morning routines."

This age group can participate more actively in the repair process, building important conflict resolution skills through your modeling.

Carlos, father of an eight-year-old, shares: "I've learned to ask my son how he experienced our conflicts rather than assuming I know. Sometimes what bothered him wasn't what I thought at all. This simple question—'What was hard for you about what happened?'—has transformed our repair conversations from my monologues to meaningful dialogues."

For Tweens and Teens (Ages 11–18)

Adolescents need repair approaches that:

- respect their increasing autonomy and perspective

- acknowledge power dynamics honestly ("As the parent, I have a greater responsibility for my communication.")

- allow for processing preferences. (Some teens need space before conversation, others need immediate connection.)

- invite genuine dialogue rather than lecture

- recognize their growing capacity for nuanced understanding

This age group needs repair that treats them as emerging adults while still providing the security of parental accountability.

Daria, mother of a 16-year-old, reflects: "The most powerful repair moment with my daughter happened when I acknowledged not just what I'd said in anger, but the pattern it represented. 'I've been critical of your choices lately instead of trusting your judgment. I'm sorry, and I'm working on that.' That level of honesty about our relationship dynamic meant more to her than any apology for a specific incident could have."

Common Repair Challenges

Even with the best intentions, repair faces obstacles. Here's how to navigate common challenges when applying these research-backed techniques:

When Emotions Remain Too Hot

Sometimes repair attempts occur before sufficient regulation, leading to escalation rather than resolution. When emotions remain highly activated:

- Extend the cooling pause: "I'm still feeling too upset to have this conversation well."

- Use physical co-regulation before verbal processing: sitting quietly together, walking outside.

- Break larger repairs into smaller steps if needed: brief acknowledgment now, fuller conversation later.

- Recognize when additional support might be needed for regulation: deep breathing together, sensory calming activities.

- Model appropriate emotional management: "I need to take care of my feelings before we talk more."

Effective repair requires basic regulation first—attempting repair while still flooded often creates secondary ruptures.

Anika, mother of two, shares: "I used to force repair conversations while still angry, which inevitably made things worse. I've learned to say, 'I want to talk about what happened, but first I need to calm my body and mind. Let's take 20 minutes apart and then try again.' That cooling period makes our repairs actually work instead of creating new problems."

When Children Resist Repair

Sometimes children reject initial repair attempts through anger, withdrawal, or dismissal. When faced with repair resistance:

- Respect their timing while maintaining repair intention: "I understand you're not ready to talk. I'll check in again later."

- Offer multiple repair modalities: verbal, written notes, symbolic gestures

- Maintain emotional stability despite rejection: "I understand you're still upset. I'm here when you're ready."

- Consider developmental factors in resistance: Younger children may need physical reconnection before conversation; adolescents may need space to process.

- Persist gently without forcing: "Repairing our connection matters to me. I'll give you space and try again later."

This resistance often reflects self-protection rather than rejection and usually diminishes with consistent, respectful repair experiences.

James, father of a 10-year-old, notes: "When I first started attempting repair with my son, he'd turn away or say 'whatever.' I learned to say, 'I hear you're not ready to talk. I'll give you some space and check in again in a little while.' Usually by the third check-in, he was ready for connection. His initial resistance was testing whether my repair attempts were genuine and persistent."

When Patterns Feel Entrenched

Sometimes, rupture patterns feel too established for simple repair. For persistent patterns:

- Acknowledge the larger pattern, not just the single incident: "I've been critical a lot lately."

- Consider professional support for entrenched dynamics: family therapy, parent coaching.

- Commit to specific, observable change: "I'm working on speaking more calmly even when frustrated."

- Create repair systems rather than relying solely on in-the-moment efforts.

- Practice self-compassion alongside accountability. Change takes time and persistence.

Entrenched patterns require consistent effort to shift, but even long-standing dynamics can change with committed repair practice.

Malik, father of teenagers, reflects: "After years of a critical communication style, a single repair wasn't enough. I acknowledged the pattern to my kids: 'I've developed a habit of focusing on what's wrong instead of what's right, and I'm working to change that.' Then I created a concrete plan—a visible reminder to notice three positive things for every correction, and regular check-ins about how I was doing. It took months of consistent effort, but our relationship dynamic has gradually transformed."

Types of Repairs Beyond Yelling

While yelling is the most common rupture that concerns parents, effective repair applies to many relationship disconnections:

Repairing Misattunement

Sometimes the rupture involves missing your child's needs or misreading their emotional state:

- Acknowledge the miss: "I didn't realize how important this was to you."

- Validate the unmet need: "No wonder you were upset when I rushed you."

- Recommit to attunement: "I want to understand what matters to you."

- Adjust your approach based on the new understanding.

These attunement repairs strengthen your child's trust in being seen and understood.

Maya, mother of a quiet six-year-old, shares: "I completely misread my son's withdrawal after school as defiance when he was actually overwhelmed. My repair wasn't about behavior but perception: 'I thought you were being difficult, but you were actually feeling overloaded. I wasn't seeing what you needed.' That acknowledgment of misattunement rebuilt his trust that I would try to understand rather than just judge."

Repairing Unfairness

Sometimes, ruptures involve inequitable treatment or unjustified consequences:

- Acknowledge the injustice specifically: "I blamed you without getting the whole story."

- Restore fairness concretely: "I'm reversing that consequence because it wasn't warranted."

- Commit to greater equity: "I'll make sure to hear all sides before making judgments."

- Model honest self-correction: "I made a mistake in how I handled that."

These fairness repairs build your child's sense of a just world and trust in your commitment to equity.

Devon, father of siblings, reflects: "I automatically assumed my older child was at fault in a conflict without investigation. My repair focused on the injustice: 'I jumped to conclusions without getting all the information. That wasn't fair to you, and I'm sorry. I'm canceling the consequence I gave, and next time I'll make sure to understand the situation before responding.' Her relief was palpable—not just about avoiding punishment, but about being treated justly."

Repairing Boundary Overstepping

Sometimes, ruptures involve violating appropriate boundaries:

- Acknowledge the specific boundary crossed: "I shared your personal story without permission."

- Validate their right to the boundary: "You deserve privacy around your own experiences."

- Recommit to respectful limits: "I'll ask before discussing your life with others."

- Explore boundary repair: "What would help make this right?"

These boundary repairs teach crucial lessons about consent, respect, and interpersonal limits.

Sophia, mother of a teenager, shares: "I violated my daughter's privacy by reading her journal, then confronted her about its contents. My repair had to acknowledge both the boundary violation and the betrayal of trust: 'I invaded your private space and broke your trust. You have a right to your own thoughts without my intrusion. I'm committed to respecting your privacy going forward.' That repair started a deeper conversation about trust and appropriate boundaries that actually strengthened our relationship."

Creating Your Family's Repair Culture

Beyond specific repair moments, you can establish a broader family culture where repair is normalized and valued:

Develop Your Personal Repair Legacy

Your repair approach is shaped by your own history:

- Reflect on how repair was handled in your childhood: Was it expected, forbidden, or inconsistent?

- Identify your repair strengths and challenges based on this history.

- Consciously choose what repair legacy you want to create for your children.

- Practice self-compassion for the repair skills you're still developing.

- Celebrate your courage in breaking intergenerational patterns when needed.

This personal reflection builds self-awareness that enhances your repair capacity.

Leila, mother of two, reflects: "I grew up in a household where adults never apologized to children—it was seen as undermining authority. Realizing I could maintain my parental role while still acknowledging mistakes was revolutionary. I'm creating a different repair legacy for my children, showing them that accountability and authority can coexist."

Establish Repair Rituals

Specific repair practices help create reliable healing patterns:

- Develop family-specific repair language: "I need a do-over" or "Can we restart?"

- Create symbolic repair traditions: the reconciliation cup of tea, the forgiveness walk.

- Designate physical spaces for repair conversations: the resolution corner, the healing chair.

- Use repair objects that hold meaning: the talking stick, the reconnection blanket.

- Build repair into daily rhythms: bedtime clearings, dinner table check-ins.

These rituals provide scaffolding that makes repair accessible even during challenging emotions.

Jackson, father of three, shares: "We created what we call 'The Bridge Back'—a specific spot on our living room couch where family members can go when they're ready to repair a conflict. Anyone can say 'I'm on the Bridge' as an invitation to reconnect. Having this designated space and language makes repair feel like a normal part of our family life rather than a special event."

Model Repair Beyond Parent-Child Dynamics

Children learn repair not just from receiving it but from observing it:

- Practice visible repair with your partner or co-parent.

- Acknowledge mistakes with other adults in your children's presence.

- Repair ruptures with siblings, friends, or extended family members.

- Discuss repair in books, movies, or current events.

- Acknowledge institutional or historical examples of repair or its absence.

This broader modeling shows children that repair is a lifelong relational skill, not just a parenting technique.

Emilya, co-parenting through divorce, notes: "One of the most powerful repair moments for our children was witnessing their father and me apologize to each other after a tense co-parenting exchange. We deliberately did this in front of them, not to burden them with adult issues, but to show that repair is possible even in complex relationships. They visibly relaxed seeing that conflict doesn't have to mean permanent disconnection."

Normalize the Repair Cycle

Creating a repair-positive environment involves shifting how the entire cycle is viewed:

- Discuss rupture and repair as normal, expected relationship processes.

- Acknowledge repair as a strength, not a weakness: "It takes courage to admit mistakes."

- Celebrate repair moments: "I appreciate how we worked through that tough moment."

- Use repair-positive language: "We had a disconnection and found our way back."

- Frame repair as evidence of relationship health rather than relationship failure.

This normalization removes shame from the repair process, making it accessible and valued.

Marcus, father of siblings, shares: "We started explicitly naming repair as a family strength. After working through conflicts, I might say, 'I love how our family knows how to reconnect after hard moments. Not every family has that superpower.' This framing has transformed repair from something shameful to something we take pride in."

Building Your Repair Ritual

Start implementing the repair ritual with these practical steps:

Develop Your Personal Repair Script

Create language for the key repair elements that feels authentic to you:

- Acknowledgment: "I spoke harshly when I was frustrated."

- Impact recognition: "I can see that scared/hurt/upset you."

- Reconnection: "I love you no matter what."

- Forward focus: "Next time I feel that way, I'll take a breath first."

Having this language prepared helps you access it even when emotionally dysregulated.

Create Environmental Repair Supports

Physical reminders help implement repair intentions:

- Post repair language in private spaces: bathroom mirror, inside a kitchen cabinet.

- Establish a repair corner with comfort items and visual prompts.

- Create repair cards with scripts for different situations.

- Designate specific objects or locations for repair conversations.

- Develop physical signals for repair readiness: special light on, specific music playing.

These environmental supports reduce cognitive load during emotional moments.

Practice Preventive Maintenance

Regular connection rituals reduce the intensity and frequency of ruptures:

- Schedule brief but regular one-on-one time with each child.

- Establish daily connection points that are protected from discipline issues.

- Create preemptive repair habits: "Is there anything we need to clear up between us?"

- Practice appreciation exchanges that strengthen the relationship foundation.

- Build regular emotional check-ins: "How's your heart feeling today?"

This preventive approach creates a relationship buffer that makes ruptures less damaging and repair more accessible.

Implement the Full Repair Sequence

When ruptures occur, follow the complete process:

1. Take the cooling pause needed for basic regulation.

2. Make clear, specific acknowledgment of your role.

3. Create reconnection through verbal and physical means as welcomed.

4. Look forward with learning rather than backward with shame.

5. Close the repair loop explicitly: "Do you feel better about what happened? Is there anything else you want me to know?"

This complete sequence transforms ruptures from relationship damage to relationship strength.

Develop Repair Flexibility

Different situations, children, and developmental stages require varied approaches:

- Create multiple repair pathways: verbal, written, playful, serious.

- Respect individual preferences for repair timing and style.

- Adjust repair depth based on rupture significance.

- Balance consistency with personalization.

- Evolve repair approaches as children develop.

This flexibility ensures repair remains accessible across changing circumstances.

The repair ritual isn't about creating perfect interactions—that's neither possible nor desirable for your child's development. It's about demonstrating that relationships can heal after disconnection, that mistakes can lead to growth rather than shame, and that love persists even through imperfect moments.

Every time you repair a rupture with your child, you're not just fixing a specific incident—you're building their fundamental trust in relationship resilience. You're showing them that human connections can bend without breaking, strengthen through challenges, and deepen through honest accountability. This lesson extends far beyond your relationship with them, shaping how they'll navigate all relationships throughout their lives.

Andrea, mother of now-adult children, reflects: "Looking back over 25 years of parenting, I believe repair might be the most important skill I taught my children. They grew up seeing that relationships can heal after conflict, that people can acknowledge mistakes without losing dignity, and that connection can be restored even after painful moments. Now I watch them navigate their adult relationships with that same repair capacity—acknowledging missteps, taking responsibility, and rebuilding bridges rather than burning them. Of all my parenting legacy, this might be what I'm most proud of."

In the next chapter, we'll explore the parent recharge plan— how to sustain yourself through the marathon of parenting so you can consistently show up as the parent you want to be.

Quick tip: After losing your cool, wait until both you and your child are regulated, then acknowledge specifically what happened: "I raised my voice when I felt frustrated." This teaches that relationships can heal after ruptures.

Repair Ritual Reflection Questions

1. What messages about repair did you receive in your family of origin?

2. Which type of rupture do you find most difficult to repair with your children?

3. What personal barriers make repair challenging for you (pride, shame, fear)?

4. What would a stronger repair culture provide for your family?

5. What's one repair you could make this week for a recent or lingering rupture?

TOOL 9:
THE PARENT RECHARGE PLAN

You've reached the final chapter of this book, exploring eight powerful tools to transform your parenting. You've learned about managing triggers, communicating respectfully, setting boundaries, engaging in meaningful conversations, managing emotions, creating effective routines, and repairing inevitable ruptures.

But there's a critical piece missing—the foundation that makes all these tools possible.

You.

Your capacity to implement everything we've discussed depends on one essential factor: your own well-being. Not in some vague "self-care is important" way, but in the concrete, neurobiological reality that you cannot consistently give what you do not have.

The parent recharge plan addresses this fundamental truth by creating sustainable practices that maintain your emotional, physical, and relational resources. This isn't a luxury or an afterthought—it's the infrastructure that powers everything else.

The Science of Parental Depletion

Research in neuropsychology has identified a condition called "parental burnout," a state of emotional, physical, and mental exhaustion caused by the chronic stress of parenting without adequate resources or recovery[18]. This state is characterized by:

- emotional distancing from children

- feeling overwhelmed by parental responsibilities

- contrast between the idealized parent you want to be and your actual parenting reality

- physical symptoms, including fatigue, sleep disturbance, and tension

- increased irritability and decreased patience

- cognitive impacts, including decision fatigue and attention problems

This burnout state isn't just unpleasant—it biologically impairs your capacity to implement positive parenting practices. When chronically depleted, your brain literally cannot access its higher functions effectively.

Dr. Stuart Shanker, self-regulation expert, explains: "A depleted nervous system defaults to its most primitive reactions. No amount of parenting knowledge can override this biological reality. The parent who wants to respond differently but keeps

---

[18] Hubert & Aujoulat, 2018

defaulting to old patterns isn't failing at implementation—their system lacks the energy required for new neural pathways."[19]

This science offers both validation and direction. The frustrating gap between what you know you should do and what you actually do in stressful moments often isn't about knowledge or motivation—it's about resource depletion. The solution isn't trying harder; it's recharging more effectively.

The Five Elements of Effective Recharging

The parent recharge plan consists of five key elements that work together to maintain the resources you need for sustainable parenting. This isn't about occasional spa days or girls' nights out—it's about building daily and weekly practices that prevent depletion rather than just responding to burnout.

The Physiological Foundation

Effective recharging begins with meeting basic biological needs that directly impact brain function:

- treating sleep as non-negotiable infrastructure

- nutrition patterns that stabilize blood sugar and energy levels

- hydration maintenance throughout the day

- movement integrated into daily rhythms, not just isolated "workouts"

---

[19] King, 2016

- sensory regulation awareness and management

This foundation isn't about perfect health habits or unrealistic wellness ideals. It's about identifying your personal physiological minimums—the baseline needs that must be met for your nervous system to function reasonably well.

Marcus, father of three young children, shares: "I was trying to be Super Dad while running on five hours of broken sleep, no breakfast, and coffee as my primary fluid. No wonder I kept losing it with my kids despite knowing better! When I finally treated my sleep as a non-negotiable parenting responsibility rather than a luxury, my capacity to use the parenting tools I knew about increased dramatically."

The Nervous System Reset

Regular practices that shift your nervous system from stress activation to restorative states are essential:

- Brief but frequent regulation breaks: two-minute breathing practices, sensory resets

- State-shifting rituals between roles and responsibilities: the after-work reset, the before-bedtime wind-down

- Nature exposure, even in small doses: the five-minute outdoor breath break, indoor plant engagement

- Sensory pleasure integration: music, texture, flavor, scent as nervous system resources

- Physical release practices: movement, vocal expression, therapeutic touch

These practices maintain your physiological capacity for regulated responses rather than reactive ones.

Sophia, mother of a child with special needs, reflects: "I created what I call 'regulation stations' throughout my house and day—tiny opportunities to reset my system. The 30 seconds of deep breathing at red lights, the lavender hand lotion I apply after stressful interactions, the 'bathroom breathing break' when tensions rise. These micro-practices maintain my capacity to be the parent I want to be, even under significant pressure."

The Connection Network

Humans are neurobiologically wired for co-regulation—our nervous systems regulate best in supportive connection with others:

- Intentional adult relationships that offer authentic exchange: leaning on others who are in the same boat

- Parenting-specific support systems: those who understand your unique challenges

- Brief but meaningful connection moments throughout the day: the five-minute check-in call, the text exchange with a friend

- Strategic vulnerability with safe others: sharing struggles as well as successes

- Reciprocal support systems: giving and receiving practical and emotional assistance

This connection network provides external regulation resources when your internal ones are depleted.

Jamal, a single father, shares: "I created what I call my 'parenting pit crew'—three other parents I can text SOS messages to when I'm struggling. Sometimes, I just need validation, sometimes tactical advice, sometimes someone to take my kids for an hour. This network has made the difference between barely surviving and actually thriving as a parent."

The Identity Maintenance

Parenthood can consume identity, leading to depletion when other aspects of self are neglected:

- preserving non-parent identity elements: professional, creative, intellectual, spiritual

- maintaining connections to pre-parent interests and activities, even in modified forms

- creating psychological space separate from parenting concerns

- protecting time for activities that generate flow states and deep engagement

- honoring values and purposes beyond family roles

This identity maintenance ensures you're refueling your unique sense of self rather than becoming depleted by role reduction.

Anika, mother of three, notes: "I nearly lost myself in early parenthood, becoming 'just Mom' and wondering where the passionate, creative person I'd been had gone. My turning point was reclaiming just twenty minutes three times a week for writing—my pre-parent passion. That small practice of maintaining my writer identity alongside my mother identity completely changed my sense of depletion. I wasn't just pouring out anymore; I was also filling up."

The Meaning Framework

Sustainable parenting requires a sense of purpose and meaning that transcends daily challenges:

- connecting parenting choices to core values and meaningful legacy

- creating rituals that highlight purpose amid mundane moments

- developing language for the deeper significance of parenting work

- building reflection practices that reveal growth and impact

- finding meaning in the struggle itself, not just in idealized outcomes

This meaning framework transforms depleting obligations into purposeful choices, even when difficult.

David, father of a child with chronic health needs, reflects: "When my daughter was diagnosed, the medical caregiving nearly broke me—constant appointments, therapies, and daily interventions on top of regular parenting. What saved me was developing a meaning framework for this work. Each night, I journal one way my presence made a difference, whether supporting her through a procedure or just creating a moment of joy amid the challenges. Connecting to purpose doesn't make the work easier, but it makes it sustainable."

Recharging Across Different Life Stages

Effective recharging adapts across changing family circumstances:

For Parents of Infants and Toddlers (Ages 0–3)

This physically intensive stage requires recharging that:

- works within severe time and sleep constraints

- leverages micro-moments rather than extended periods

- addresses intense physical depletion: Touch saturation, sleep deprivation

- creates tag-team systems with partners or support people when possible

- lowers standards temporarily in non-essential areas to preserve energy

The key is preventing complete depletion rather than waiting for ideal recharge conditions.

Marla, mother of an infant and toddler, shares: "I had to abandon my pre-baby idea that self-care meant an hour of yoga or a long bath. I created what I call 'minute meditations'—60 seconds of deep breathing while the water boils, 2 minutes of stretching while supervising bath time, 30 seconds of stepping outside for three deep breaths. These micro-practices maintained just enough regulation capacity to get through the hardest phases."

For Parents of School-Age Children (Ages 4–12)

This logistically complex stage benefits from recharging that:

- creates systems that reduce decision fatigue and mental load

- establishes boundaries around children's activities and parent involvement

- builds parent network support for practical assistance

- protects dedicated identity maintenance time

- develops clear on-duty/off-duty delineations with co-parents

The focus shifts from physical survival to managing the complex mental and emotional demands of this stage.

Carlos, father of three elementary students, explains: "I was drowning in logistics—forms, schedules, homework supervision, social coordination. My breakthrough came when I created systems instead of handling each thing individually. We have a dedicated form-processing day, a centralized family calendar, and alternating 'parent off-duty' evenings where my wife and I each get one night per week of zero parenting responsibility after dinner."

For Parents of Adolescents (Ages 13–18)

This emotionally demanding stage requires recharging that:

- addresses the complex feelings triggered by teenage development

- creates emotional processing outlets for parental worries and fears

- maintains appropriate boundaries as teens push for independence

- builds support networks specific to adolescent parenting challenges

- begins transition planning for post-intensive parenting phases

The emphasis becomes maintaining emotional resilience through significant relationship evolution.

Evelyn, mother of two teenagers, reflects: "Parenting teens requires emotional stamina more than physical energy. I found I needed regular processing spaces—both therapy and close friendships, where I could express the complex grief, pride, fear, and joy of watching my children individuate. Having places to authentically share these feelings prevents them from spilling into my parenting interactions in unhelpful ways."

Common Recharging Obstacles

Even with understanding and intention, parents face significant challenges in implementing effective recharging. Here's how to navigate common obstacles:

When Time Seems Absolutely Impossible

In seasons where time feels completely consumed by obligations:

- Focus on recharging quality over quantity: 5 minutes of genuine restoration vs. 30 minutes of distracted "self-care."

- Integrate recharging into existing activities: mindful awareness during shower time, deep breathing during commute.

- Leverage transition moments between activities for micro-resets.

- Identify and eliminate non-essential time drains: Social media scrolling, unnecessary perfectionism.

- Create "good enough" thresholds for tasks to prevent time overconsumption.

The key is shifting from an "available time" mindset to a "necessary infrastructure" mindset.

Sara, mother of four, including a child with special needs, shares: "I literally scheduled three-minute breaks in my day—setting a timer, closing my eyes, breathing deeply, and visualizing a peaceful place. These microscopic pauses maintained just enough regulation capacity to prevent complete depletion. The mindset shift was treating these moments as non-negotiable infrastructure rather than indulgences."

When Financial Resources Are Limited

When economic pressures create additional barriers:

- Focus on no-cost regulation practices: breathing techniques, free nature access, body movement.

159

- Create resource-sharing systems with other families: childcare exchanges, meal preparation rotations.

- Identify community resources designed for family support.

- Distinguish between luxury indulgences and genuine needs.

- Advocate for workplace policies that support family well-being.

Effective recharging requires resources but can be adapted to various economic realities.

Michael, a father working multiple jobs, notes: "I can't afford expensive self-care or childcare. My recharge plan includes meeting another dad and our kids at the park—the kids play while we take turns having 15 minutes to just sit or take a walk alone. It costs nothing but maintains my sanity. I've also learned to use my commute time for deep breathing and setting intentions rather than worrying about bills."

When Support Systems Are Minimal

For parents with limited practical support:

- Prioritize building even one or two reliable support connections.

- Create virtual support through online communities with similar circumstances.

- Develop extremely clear boundaries around truly essential activities.

- Lower standards strategically in areas less critical to well-being.

- Identify professional resources designed for your specific situation.

Limited support requires greater intentionality about resource allocation but doesn't make recharging impossible.

Lily, a single parent in a new city, shares: "When we relocated, I had zero local support. I created what I call my 'virtual village'—an online group of single parents who text daily and video chat weekly. We problem-solve together, validate struggles, and provide emotional support even when practical help isn't possible. This connection has been crucial to maintaining my capacity to parent well despite minimal in-person support."

When Guilt Blocks Recharging

Internal barriers often prove more challenging than external ones:

- Recognize guilt as information, not a command to ignore needs.

- Distinguish between unnecessary indulgence and necessary infrastructure.

- Connect recharging directly to improved family outcomes.

- Challenge beliefs about parental sacrifice as inherently virtuous.

- Build a network that normalizes and encourages appropriate self-care.

The mindset shift from "selfish luxury" to "necessary maintenance" transforms the guilt narrative.

James, father of a child with behavioral challenges, reflects: "I used to feel guilty taking even 30 minutes for exercise, believing any time for myself was time stolen from my son, who needed constant support. My perspective shifted when our family therapist reframed it: 'Your regulation is his regulation. Your self-care is his therapy.' That connected my needs directly to his well-being, making it easier to prioritize without guilt."

Building Your Personal Recharge System

Start implementing the parent recharge plan with these practical steps:

Conduct a Depletion Audit

Before creating a recharge plan, assess your current state:

1. Track your energy levels throughout the day for one week.

2. Identify your personal depletion warning signs: Irritability, withdrawal, specific physical symptoms.

3. Notice which parenting scenarios consistently deplete your resources.

4. Distinguish between physical, emotional, and cognitive depletion patterns.

5. Recognize the gap between your capacity on well-resourced versus depleted days.

This assessment provides crucial information about your specific recharge needs.

Identify Your Minimum Viable Recharge

Determine the absolute baseline practices required for reasonable function:

- Sleep requirements: hours and quality needed for basic regulation

- Nutrition foundations: eating patterns that stabilize your energy and mood

- Movement minimums: activity types and frequency for your body's needs

- Connection essentials: relationship interactions that sustain your emotional health

- Solitude requirements: alone time needed for your particular temperament

This minimum viable recharge becomes your non-negotiable foundation.

Create Environmental Recharge Supports

Design your physical environment to support recharging:

- Establish regulation stations throughout your home: breathing reminder notes, calming sensory items.

- Remove friction from essential recharge activities: exercise clothes laid out, healthy snacks prepared.

- Create visual reminders of recharge priorities: calendar blocks, bathroom mirror notes.

- Reduce environmental aspects that deplete resources: clutter, excessive noise, disruptive technology.

- Designate specific recharge spaces, even if small: the meditation corner, the reading chair.

These environmental scaffolds make recharging more accessible during depleted states.

Develop Your Support Network

Intentionally build the connections that sustain you:

- Identify existing relationships that offer genuine support.

- Be specific about what types of support you need most.

- Create reciprocal arrangements that benefit all parties.

- Establish clear communication systems for asking for help.

- Build both emergency support and maintenance support connections.

This network transforms parenting from an isolated endeavor to a community-supported role.

Schedule System Maintenance

Create regular practices to assess and adjust your recharge system:

- weekly brief check-ins to identify developing depletion patterns

- monthly deeper reviews of what's working and what needs adjustment

- seasonal reassessment as family needs and schedules change

- annual bigger-picture evaluation of overall sustainability

- ongoing adaptation to developmental changes in children and parents

This maintenance prevents complete system failure by catching depletion patterns early.

The parent recharge plan isn't about achieving some idealized work-life balance or perfect self-care routine. It's about creating sustainable practices that maintain the minimum resources you need to be the parent you want to be. Some seasons will allow for more abundant recharging, while others will require focusing on just the essential minimum. The key is treating your well-being as necessary infrastructure rather than an optional luxury.

Kelly, mother of now-adult children, reflects on two decades of parenting: "Looking back, I realize that the quality of my parenting directly correlated with how well I maintained my own resources. The times I showed up as the parent I wanted to be weren't when I sacrificed everything for my kids—those periods actually led to my worst parenting moments. My best parenting emerged when I maintained enough sleep, supportive connections, and practices that honored my own humanity alongside my children's needs. If I could tell new parents one thing, it would be this: Your children don't need your sacrifice. They need your sustained presence, and that requires taking care of yourself."

Conclusion: From Tools to Transformation

As we conclude our journey through these nine tools, remember that transformation isn't about perfect implementation. It's about consistent progress in the direction of your values. Every time you use your reset button instead of yelling, engage your respect loop instead of demanding, implement your calm script instead of threatening, or repair after an inevitable rupture, you're rewiring both your brain and your relationship with your child.

The path isn't linear. You'll have days of beautiful connection followed by complete regression into old patterns. You'll nail the emotional coaching in one moment and completely miss the mark in the next. This inconsistency isn't failure—it's the normal, messy process of human growth and relationship.

What matters isn't perfection but persistence. Each time you return to these tools, the neural pathways strengthen. Each repair builds trust that ruptures aren't fatal to connection. Each self-regulation attempt increases your capacity for the next challenge.

Parenthood isn't about achieving some idealized state of perpetual patience and wisdom. It's about showing up authentically in the ongoing dance of connection, growth, rupture, and repair. It's about being human with other humans who happen to be smaller and still developing.

The tools in this book aren't meant to transform you into a perfect parent. They're meant to help you become more consistently the parent you already want to be—one who connects rather than controls, who guides rather than demands, who repairs rather than persists in patterns that damage connection.

You already have everything you need for this journey. The love that led you to pick up this book is the same love that will fuel your continued growth, even when it's difficult. Your desire to do better isn't evidence of failure—it's the foundation of transformation.

Parent yourself with the same compassion you aspire to parent your children. Acknowledge your efforts, forgive your missteps, and trust the process of growth. The fact that you've read this far demonstrates your commitment to becoming the parent your children need.

You've got this. Not perfectly, but persistently. And that persistence, not perfection, is what will ultimately transform your family.

Quick tip: Identify your personal depletion warning signs—irritability, physical tension, decision fatigue—and treat your minimum recharge needs as non-negotiable parenting infrastructure, not optional self-indulgence.

Parent Recharge Reflection Questions

1. What are your earliest warning signs of parental depletion?

2. Which aspect of recharging do you find most challenging to prioritize?

3. What's one small recharge practice you could implement this week?

4. Who makes up your current support network, and what gaps exist?

5. How might your parenting capacity expand with more consistent recharging?

CONCLUSION

You've made it to the end of our journey together, exploring nine powerful tools that can transform your relationship with your children. But in many ways, this isn't an ending—it's a beginning. The real work starts now, in the day-to-day moments of implementation, practice, stumbling, getting up again, and gradually rewiring both your brain and your family dynamics.

Let me share something important: I still yell sometimes. Yes, even as the author of a book called *Talk, Don't Yell*. Perfect implementation of these tools isn't the goal, because perfection isn't possible. What's possible—and what matters far more—is progress. Each time you pause before reacting, each time you repair after a rupture, each time you prioritize connection over control, you're strengthening new neural pathways that eventually become your default response.

Change happens through repetition, not perfection. Every time you choose a tool from this book instead of defaulting to old patterns, you're building stronger connections in your brain that make those choices easier next time. The parent who uses the reset button successfully once a week is making genuine progress. The parent who tries the emotional coach approach and fumbles through it imperfectly is still teaching their child something invaluable—that emotions matter and can be managed.

These tools aren't about transforming you into some idealized "perfect parent." They're about helping you become more consistently the parent you already want to be—one who creates security through boundaries, connection through respect, and resilience through repair.

Remember that your children don't need a perfect parent. They need a real one—someone who makes mistakes and shows them how to recover, someone who has bad days but demonstrates how to reset, someone who struggles with big feelings but models managing them. Your willingness to grow is teaching them something far more valuable than perfection ever could.

As you move forward, be gentle with yourself. Recognize that implementation happens in stages:

- First comes awareness—noticing the patterns and triggers that lead to yelling.

- Then comes interruption—catching yourself mid-pattern and creating a pause. Next is substitution— trying a different approach, even if imperfectly.

- Finally comes integration, when new patterns begin to feel natural and automatic.

These stages don't progress linearly. You'll have periods of beautiful growth followed by days when you seem to forget everything you've learned. That's not failure—it's being human.

The only real failure would be giving up on the journey altogether.

You're doing important work—perhaps the most important work there is. You're healing patterns that may have persisted through generations. You're creating new possibilities for your children and the families they may someday build. You're proving that change is possible, even in the most challenging circumstances.

Take these tools and use them imperfectly. Celebrate small victories. Repair when you miss the mark. Rest when you're depleted. Reach out for support when you need it. And trust that every effort, no matter how small, creates ripples of positive change that extend far beyond what you can see.

You've got this—not perfectly, but persistently. And in the end, that persistent effort toward connection, respect, and regulation is what your children will remember and carry forward. That's the legacy that matters most.

Thank you for joining me on this journey. I'm honored to be part of your story, and I believe in your capacity to create the family life you envision—one imperfect, beautiful day at a time.

Bonus Materials

Daily Tool Selector

Choosing the right parenting tool in challenging moments can be difficult, especially when emotions run high. Use this decision tree to quickly identify which approach might work best for the situation you're facing.

Decision Tree for Parenting Challenges

Start here: What's happening right now?

I'm feeling triggered and about to yell → Use Tool 1: The Reset Button

- Take a deep breath.

- Name your emotion internally: "I'm feeling frustrated."

- Use a physical pattern interrupt: press feet into floor, shoulders down.

- Only proceed when your nervous system has regulated enough for conscious choice.

My child and I are stuck in a respect problem → Use Tool 2: The Respect Loop

- Model the respect you want to see first.

- Use the same tone you'd use with a respected colleague.

- Repair quickly if you slip into disrespectful communication.

- Remember: Children learn respect by experiencing it, not by being demanded to show it.

I need to communicate a limit or request → Use Tool 3: The Calm Script

- Connect before correcting: "I see you're having fun with that game..."

- Make your request clear and specific: "It's time to put the iPad away for dinner."

- Validate feelings while maintaining the boundary: "I know it's disappointing *and* it's time to stop."

- Follow through calmly if needed: "I'll help you find a stopping point."

I need to establish or maintain a boundary → Use Tool 4: The Boundary Builder

- Clarify the boundary in specific, behavioral terms.

- Connect before stating the boundary.

- Commit to consistency in enforcement.

- Consider the developmental appropriateness of your expectations.

I want my child to open up about their day/feelings → Use Tool 5: The Conversation Catcher

- Create side-by-side opportunities for talking.

- Use open-ended questions rather than interrogations.

- Show curiosity without judgment.

- Allow for comfortable silence rather than filling every gap.

My child is experiencing big emotions → Use Tool 6: The Emotional Coach

- Validate the feeling: "You're feeling really disappointed."

- Normalize the emotion: "That makes sense. Anyone would feel that way."

- Offer support: "Would you like a hug or some space?"

- Problem-solve only after emotional processing: "When you're ready, we can figure out what to do next."

We're stuck in daily power struggles around routines → Use Tool 7: The Routine Reset

- Assess where structural friction points exist.

- Create visual supports for expectations.

- Build in connection points within routines.

- Balance structure with appropriate autonomy.

I messed up and need to repair the relationship → Use Tool 8: The Repair Ritual

- Take a cooling pause if needed.

- Acknowledge your part specifically without justifications.

- Rebuild connection through reassurance and physical touch if welcomed.

- Move forward with learning rather than lingering in guilt.

I'm feeling depleted and struggling to use any tools → Use Tool 9: The Parent Recharge Plan

- Identify your minimum viable recharge needs.

- Take even micro-moments for regulation.

- Connect with supportive others.

- Remember: Your capacity to parent well depends on your well-being.

Quick Reference Guide for Common Challenges

Morning Chaos
- Primary tool: the routine reset

- Supporting tools: the calm script, the reset button

- Key strategy: Design your routine to require minimal parental supervision, using visual supports and prepping the night before.

Homework Resistance

- Primary tool: the boundary builder

- Supporting tools: the emotional coach, the respect loop

- Key strategy: Establish clear expectations while validating frustrations; focus on creating the proper environmental conditions.

Bedtime Battles

- Primary tool: the routine reset

- Supporting tools: the calm script, the connection catcher

- Key strategy: Create a consistent sequence with decreasing stimulation and built-in connection moments.

Sibling Fighting

- Primary tool: the emotional coach

- Supporting tools: the respect loop, the boundary builder

- Key strategy: Help each child process emotions before problem-solving; focus on teaching skills rather than assigning blame.

Public Meltdowns

- Primary tool: the reset button (for you), the emotional coach (for them)

- Supporting tools: the repair ritual (if needed afterward)

- Key strategy: Prioritize co-regulation over behavior management; remember that your calm is contagious.

Technology Transitions

- Primary tool: the boundary builder

- Supporting tools: the calm script, the routine reset

- Key strategy: Set clear time boundaries with visual cues; give transition warnings; establish consistent consequences.

Defiance and Backtalk

- Primary tool: the respect loop

- Supporting tools: the calm script, the repair ritual

- Key strategy: Model respectful communication even when challenged; address the behavior without attacking the child's character.

Sibling Conflict Resolution Guide

Sibling relationships offer children their first laboratory for resolving conflicts, negotiating, and regulating emotions with peers. Your guidance can transform these conflicts from family disruptions into valuable learning opportunities.

Adapting the Nine Tools for Multiple Children

The Reset Button for Sibling Conflicts

- Use your reset first before addressing the children.

- Model calm in the storm of sibling emotions.

- Recognize that sibling triggers may be especially potent for you based on your own childhood experiences.

- Remember that your regulation affects all children involved.

The Respect Loop for Siblings

- Avoid taking sides or labeling children as "victim" and "aggressor."

- Use respectful language even when describing problematic behaviors.

- Demonstrate respectful listening to each child's perspective.

- Create family respect agreements that apply to all relationships.

The Calm Script for Sibling Interventions

- Address each child individually rather than as a unit.

- Use neutral, descriptive language about what you observe.

- Avoid comparative language that ranks or compares siblings.

- Maintain the same calm tone regardless of which child you're addressing.

The Boundary Builder for Sibling Dynamics

- Establish clear interpersonal boundaries: "Bodies are never for hurting."

- Differentiate between shared resources and personal property.

- Create visual reminders of sibling boundaries.

- Enforce boundaries consistently regardless of which child crossed them.

The Conversation Catcher for Sibling Relationships

- Create individual connection time with each child.

- Use communication tools like talking sticks for family discussions.

- Ask future-focused questions: "How would you like things to be different?"

- Listen without immediately trying to solve or judge.

The Emotional Coach for Sibling Feelings

- Validate competing feelings without choosing sides.

- Help siblings recognize emotions in each other.

- Teach emotional vocabulary for complex sibling feelings: jealousy, comparison, identity.

- Support each child's distinct emotional needs within the same situation.

The Routine Reset for Multiple Children

- Design routines that minimize sibling friction points.

- Create individual zones and simultaneous activities when needed.

- Build in paired activities that foster positive sibling interaction.

- Adjust routines to account for different developmental stages.

The Repair Ritual for Sibling Ruptures

- Facilitate sibling repairs without forcing apologies.

- Model repair between you and each child.

- Create family-specific repair rituals that siblings can initiate.

- Celebrate successful repairs as relationship-strengthening.

The Parent Recharge Plan With Multiple Children

- Recognize the increased risk of depletion with multiple children.

- Create "divide and conquer" strategies with co-parents.

- Build in transition support between individual child connections.

- Protect energy for fair distribution among children.

Special Considerations for Sibling Dynamics

Birth Order and Development

- Avoid "oldest should know better" messaging.

- Recognize the developmental capabilities of each child.

- Create age-appropriate expectations for conflict resolution.

- Support identity development beyond sibling relationships.

Temperament Differences

- Honor different regulatory needs during conflicts.

- Support introverted and extroverted processing styles.

- Recognize sensory triggers between siblings.

- Adapt emotional coaching to each child's temperament.

Fairness vs. Equity

- Explain the difference between equal and equitable treatment.

- Address comparison and perceived favoritism directly.

- Create language for discussing individual needs.

- Celebrate each child's unique contributions and challenges.

Relational Skills Development

- Use conflicts as opportunities to teach negotiation

- Build empathy through perspective-taking questions

- Develop a shared language for problem-solving

- Gradually transfer conflict resolution skills to children

Co-Parent Alignment Worksheet

Consistent implementation between caregivers creates security for children and reduces confusion. This worksheet helps align approaches while respecting different parenting styles.

Creating Common Ground

Values Assessment

- What are the 3–5 most important values we want to instill in our children?

- For each value, what specific behaviors demonstrate this value?

- How will we know if we're successful in transmitting these values?

- Which values require absolute consistency between caregivers?

Boundary Consensus

- Which boundaries are non-negotiable for safety reasons?

- Which boundaries are preference-based and can vary from caregiver to caregiver?

- What are our agreed-upon consequences for boundary crossing?

- How will we communicate boundary changes to each other and the children?

Communication Protocol

- How will we address disagreements away from the children?

- What signal will we use if we need to discuss an approach in the moment?

- How frequently will we check in about our parenting alignment?

- What language will we use to support each other's decisions with the children?

Tool Implementation Agreement

- Which of the nine tools do we both feel comfortable using?

- Which tools might need modification based on our parenting styles?

- How will we communicate which tool we're using in a situation?

- How can we support each other's growth in using new approaches?

Communication Templates for Parenting Partners

- **Private concern expression:** "I noticed something I'd like to discuss about how we handled ___. When would be a good time to talk about this privately?"

- **In-the-moment support request:** "I'm working on using The Calm Script here. Could you help by giving me a moment to implement it?"

- **Alignment check-in:** "I think we might have different perspectives on ___. Can we discuss our approach so we're presenting a united front?"

- **Appreciative observation:** "I noticed how you used ___ with our child. That was really effective, and I appreciate your commitment to our shared approach."

- **Growth acknowledgment:** "I know ___ is challenging for you, and I see how hard you're working to implement this new approach. Thank you."

- **Boundary reinforcement:** "We agreed that ___ is a family rule. I need your support in maintaining this boundary consistently."

- **Repair modeling:** "I made a mistake in how I handled ___. I'm going to repair with our child and would appreciate your support as I do this."

"Say This, Not That" Yelling Replacement Cards

Instead of: "How many times do I have to tell you to pick up your toys?!"

- **Try this:** "I notice toys on the floor. They need to be in the bin before dinner."

Instead of: "Stop fighting *right now* or I'm taking everything away!"

- **Try this:** "I see two kids having a problem. Let's take a breath and then find a solution."

Instead of: "Why can't you just listen?! I'm so tired of repeating myself!"

- **Try this:** "I notice I've said this several times. That tells me we need a different approach."

Instead of: "That's it! No screens for a week! I've had enough!"

- **Try this:** "I'm feeling frustrated right now. I need a moment to calm down before we discuss consequences."

Instead of: "You're going to be late *again*! Can't you move any faster?!"

- **Try this:** "I notice we're running behind schedule. What's one thing I could do to help you move more quickly?"

Instead of: "Your room is a complete disaster! How can you live like this?!"

- **Try this:** "I notice your room needs attention. Let's set a 10-minute timer and clean together."

Instead of: "Why would you do that?! What were you thinking?!"

- **Try this:** "I see what happened. I'm curious about what was going on for you when you made that choice."

Instead of: "If you don't stop that right now, you'll be sorry!"

- **Try this:** "That behavior isn't working for our family. You can choose to stop now or take a break to reset."

Parent Recharge Checklist

Daily Essentials
☐ 3 deep breaths before getting out of bed

☐ hydration (water bottle filled and accessible)

☐ protein-containing breakfast

☐ 5 minutes of solo time (even if it's in the bathroom!)

☐ 30 seconds of outdoor air/natural light

☐ 3 moments of conscious presence with my child

☐ brief connection with another adult (text, call, conversation)

Weekly Priorities
☐ 1 hour of complete parenting relief (partner, childcare, swap)

☐ physical movement that feels good in my body

☐ connection with supportive adult(s) who understand parenting challenges

☐ activity that connects to non-parent identity (hobby, interest, skill)

☐ intentional pleasure experience (sensory enjoyment, creativity, play)

☐ system review and adjustment (what's working/not working?)

☐ gratitude reflection (what went well this week?)

Depletion Warning Signs

☐ increased irritability over minor issues

☐ feeling resentful toward family members

☐ physical symptoms (headaches, tension, fatigue)

☐ emotional numbness or disconnection

☐ fantasizing about escape scenarios

☐ decreased patience for normal child behaviors

☐ difficulty making simple decisions

Emergency Recharge Interventions

☐ Take a 60-second bathroom breathing break.

☐ Text SOS to support person.

☐ Put on uplifting music and move your body.

☐ Step outside for 3 minutes of fresh air.

☐ Drink water and eat protein.

☐ Reduce sensory input (dim lights, reduce noise).

☐ Implement "parallel play" time where everyone does their own activity.

Emotional Regulation Visual Cards

For Children: "How Do I Feel?" Emotional Awareness Cards

- Happy (smiling face): My body feels light and warm.

- Sad (tearful face): My body feels heavy and slow.

- Angry (frowning face with furrowed brow): My body feels hot and tight.

- Worried (wide-eyed concerned face): My body feels shaky and jumpy.

- Calm (peaceful face): My body feels steady and relaxed.

- Excited (enthusiastic face): My body feels bouncy and energetic.

- Frustrated (grimacing face): My body feels stuck and tense.

- Safe (contented face): My body feels warm and peaceful.

For Children: "What Can I Do?" Regulation Strategy Cards

- Deep belly breaths: Place a hand on your belly and breathe slowly.

- Physical movement: Jump, dance, or run to release energy.

- Sensory comfort: Squeeze a stress ball or hug a stuffed animal.

- Quiet space: Go to the calm corner for a few minutes alone.

- Talk about it: Find a trusted person to share your feelings.

- Count to 10: Give your brain time to calm down.

- Ask for help: It's okay to need support with big feelings.

- Draw your feelings: Express emotions through art.

For Parents: "Regulation Red Flags" Awareness Cards

- Raised voice: Your volume is increasing.

- Physical tension: Your shoulders, jaw, or hands are tight.

- Accelerated speech: Your words are coming faster.

- Emotional language: You're using absolutes like "always" or "never."

- Tunnel vision: You're focused only on the problem behavior.

- Threatening posture: Your body is looming or aggressive.

- Mental catastrophizing: You're thinking, *This will never change.*

- Emotional reasoning: You're thinking, *I feel overwhelmed, so this situation is overwhelming.*

For Parents: "Reset Technique" Cards

- Physical pattern interrupt: Change your posture, unclench your hands.

- Sensory shift: Touch something with texture, focus on a distant object.

- Vocal reset: Deliberately lower your voice, slow your speech.

- Mental mantra: "This is temporary" or "I can handle this moment."

- Self-compassion: "This is hard. What do I need right now?"

- Perspective shift: "How important will this be in five years?"

- Connection reminder: "My relationship with my child matters more than this issue."

- Values check: "What kind of parent do I want to be in this moment?"

Boundary-Setting Worksheets

Step 1: Identify the Boundary Need

- What behavior is creating problems?

- Who is affected by this behavior?

- What values does this behavior impact?

- Is this a safety boundary, a respect boundary, or a preference boundary?

Step 2: Clarify the Boundary

- Write the boundary in specific, behavioral terms:

- Frame positively (what to do) rather than negatively (what not to do):

- Consider developmental appropriateness:

- Define any necessary consequences clearly:

Step 3: Plan the Communication

- Connection before correction:

- Acknowledgment of feelings/desires:

- Clear boundary statement:

- Acceptable alternatives:

- Follow-through plan:

Step 4: Evaluate Effectiveness

- Is the boundary clear to everyone involved?

- Is the boundary consistently enforced?

- Does the boundary address the underlying need?

- Does the boundary need adjustment based on implementation?

9 Tools Quick Reference Guide

Tool 1: The Reset Button

- **What:** a system for managing your triggers before they manage you

- **When to use:** when you feel yourself becoming emotionally dysregulated

- **Key phrases:** "I need a moment to reset." "I'm going to take a deep breath." "I notice I'm feeling triggered."

Tool 2: The Respect Loop

- **What:** a framework for modeling the behavior you want to see

- **When to use:** in all interactions, especially when teaching new behaviors

- **Key phrases:** "I'll speak to you respectfully, even when I'm frustrated." "In our family, we use kind words." "I made a mistake in how I spoke to you."

Tool 3: The Calm Script

- **What:** a communication approach that builds cooperation

- **When to use:** when making requests or giving directions

- **Key phrases:** "I notice you're..." "It's time to..." "I understand you feel... AND we need to..." "You can choose..."

Tool 4: The Boundary Builder

What: a system for creating and maintaining loving limits

When to use: when establishing or reinforcing family expectations

Key phrases: "In our family, we..." "This is a safety rule." "I'll help you respect this boundary." "This isn't a punishment—it's a boundary."

Tool 5: The Conversation Catcher

- **What:** techniques for creating a safe space for authentic communication

- **When to use:** when you want to encourage sharing and connection

- **Key phrases:** "I'm curious about..." "Tell me more about that." "What was that like for you?" "I'm here whenever you want to talk."

Tool 6: The Emotional Coach

- **What:** a process for helping children understand and manage feelings

- **When to use:** when your child is experiencing difficult emotions

- **Key phrases:** "You seem..." "It makes sense you feel..." "All feelings are okay." "When you're ready, we can figure out what might help."

Tool 7: The Routine Reset

What: a system for designing days that prevent chaos

When to use: when family transitions create consistent stress

Key phrases: "What's our next step in the routine?" "Let's check the schedule." "This is different today because..." "Our routine helps everyone know what to expect."

Tool 8: The Repair Ritual

- **What:** a framework for rebuilding connection after ruptures

- **When to use:** after conflicts, mistakes, or disconnection

- **Key phrases:** "I made a mistake when I..." "How did that feel for you?" "I love you even when I'm upset." "Next time, I'll try to..."

Tool 9: The Parent Recharge Plan

- **What:** a system for maintaining your emotional resources

- **When to use:** Proactively before depletion, reactively when struggling

- **Key phrases:** "I need to take care of myself so I can take care of you." "My battery is getting low." "I'm going to recharge so I can be the parent you deserve."

THANK YOU

I truly appreciate you taking the time to read this book. I hope it brought you value, sparked some new ideas, or simply gave you a fresh perspective.

If you enjoyed it, I'd be incredibly grateful if you could leave a quick review on Amazon. Your feedback not only helps others discover the book, but it also means a lot to me personally.

Thanks again for being a part of this journey.

References

Bennet, D., Bennet, A., & Turner, R. (2015, October 1). *Expanding the Self: The Intelligent Complex Adaptive Learning System (A New Theory of Adult Learning).* https://www.researchgate.net/publication/28282981 5_Expanding_the_Self_The_Intelligent_Complex_Adaptiv e_Learning_System_A_New_Theory_of_Adult_Learning

Cooke Douglas, A. (2021). *Meeting children where they are: The neurosequential model of therapeutics.* National Council for Adoption. https://adoptioncouncil.org/publications/meeting-children-where-they-are-the-neurosequential-model-of-therapeutics/

Grupe, D. W., & Nitschke, J. B. (2013). Uncertainty and anticipation in anxiety: an integrated neurobiological and psychological perspective. *Nature Reviews Neuroscience, 14*(7), 488–501. https://doi.org/10.1038/nrn3524

Hubert, S., & Aujoulat, I. (2018). Parental Burnout: When Exhausted Mothers Open Up. *Frontiers in Psychology, 9.* https://doi.org/10.3389/fpsyg.2018.01021

King, B. J. (2016, July 7). *Why It's "Self-Reg," Not Self-Control, That Matters Most For Kids.* KYUK. https://www.kyuk.org/2016-07-07/why-its-self-reg-not-self-control-that-matters-most-for-kids

Levy-Gigi, E., & Shamay-Tsoory, S. (2022). Affect labeling: The role of timing and intensity. *PLOS ONE*, *17*(12), e0279303. https://doi.org/10.1371/journal.pone.0279303

Li, T., Horta, M., Mascaro, J. S., Bijanki, K., Arnal, L. H., Adams, M., Barr, R. G., & Rilling, J. K. (2018). Explaining individual variation in paternal brain responses to infant cries. *Physiology & Behavior*, *193*, 43–54. https://doi.org/10.1016/j.physbeh.2017.12.033

López-Martínez, P., Montero-Montero, D., Moreno-Ruiz, D., & Martínez-Ferrer, B. (2019). The Role of Parental Communication and Emotional Intelligence in Child-to-Parent Violence. *Behavioral Sciences*, *9*(12), 148. https://doi.org/10.3390/bs9120148

National Collaborating Centre for Mental Health (UK). (2015, November). *Introduction to children's attachment*. National Library of Medicine; National Institute for Health and Care Excellence (UK). https://www.ncbi.nlm.nih.gov/books/NBK356196/

Rymanowicz, K. (2015, March 30). *Monkey see, monkey do: Model behavior in early childhood*. MSU Extension; Michigan State University. https://www.canr.msu.edu/news/monkey_see_monkey_do_model_behavior_in_early_childhood

Siegel, D. (2021). *Interpersonal Neurobiology*. Dr. Dan Siegel. https://drdansiegel.com/interpersonal-neurobiology/

Singer, J. (2014). *Adolescence, the Age of Opportunity: Interview with Laurence Steinberg, Ph.D.* Blogspot.com.

https://socialworkpodcast.blogspot.com/2014/09/stei
nberg.html

Tomaso, C. C., Johnson, A. B., & Nelson, T. D. (2020). The Effect of Sleep Deprivation and Restriction on Mood, Emotion, and Emotion Regulation: Three Meta-Analyses in One. *Sleep*, *44*(6). https://doi.org/10.1093/sleep/zsaa289

Veldhuis, T. M., Gordijn, E. H., Veenstra, R., & Lindenberg, S. (2014). Vicarious Group-Based Rejection: Creating a Potentially Dangerous Mix of Humiliation, Powerlessness, and Anger. *PLoS ONE*, *9*(4), e95421. https://doi.org/10.1371/journal.pone.0095421

Wang, M.-T., & Kenny, S. (2013). Longitudinal Links Between Fathers' and Mothers' Harsh Verbal Discipline and Adolescents' Conduct Problems and Depressive Symptoms. *Child Development*, *85*(3), 908–923. https://doi.org/10.1111/cdev.12143

Made in United States
North Haven, CT
16 June 2025

69834415R00114